Reading and Note Taking Guide Level B

California
Focus on
Physical Science

Boston, Massachusetts
Upper Saddle River, New Jersey

To the Teacher
This Reading and Note Taking Guide helps your students succeed in their study of science. Working through the exercises will help them understand and organize the concepts presented in the textbook. The completed worksheets then become easy-to-follow study guides for test preparation.

This Reading and Note Taking Guide also helps students improve their study and reading skills. The section "Your Keys to Success" on pages 5–10 of this Guide describes English/Language Arts skills developed in the textbook. Distribute copies of this section for students to use as a reference when completing the worksheets. Students will find it a handy tool for becoming successful readers in science and other subjects.

ISBN 0-13-203446-8

1 2 3 4 5 6 7 8 9 10 09 08 07 06 05

Contents
Physical Science

Your Keys to Success 5

Unit 1 Chemical Building Blocks

Chapter 1 Introduction to Physical Science

Section 1 What Is Physical Science? 11
Section 2 Scientific Inquiry 14
Section 3 Measurement 19
Section 4 Mathematics and Science 25
Section 5 Graphs in Science 29
Section 6 Science Laboratory Safety 34

Chapter 2 The Nature of Matter

Section 1 Describing Matter 37
Section 2 Changes in Matter 42
Section 3 Energy and Matter 44

Chapter 3 Solids, Liquids, and Gases

Section 1 States of Matter 46
Section 2 Changes of State 50
Section 3 The Behavior of Gases 53

Chapter 4 Elements and the Periodic Table

Section 1 Introduction to Atoms 57
Section 2 Organizing the Elements 61
Section 3 Metals 65
Section 4 Nonmetals, Inert Gases, and Semimetals 69
Section 5 Radioactive Elements 73

Unit 2 Chemical Interactions

Chapter 5 Atoms and Bonding

Section 1 Atoms, Bonding, and the Periodic Table 77
Section 2 Ionic Bonds 80
Section 3 Covalent Bonds 84
Section 4 Bonding in Metals 88

Chapter 6 Chemical Reactions

Section 1 Observing Chemical Change 92
Section 2 Describing Chemical Reactions 95
Section 3 Controlling Chemical Reactions 100
Section 4 Fire and Fire Safety 104

Chapter 7 Acids, Bases, and Solutions

Section 1 Understanding Solutions 106
Section 2 Concentration and Solubility 110
Section 3 Describing Acids and Bases 113
Section 4 Acids and Bases in Solution 116

Chapter 8 Carbon Chemistry

Section 1 Properties of Carbon 119
Section 2 Carbon Compounds 121
Section 3 Polymers and Composites 128
Section 4 Life With Carbon 131

Unit 3 Motion, Forces, and Energy

Chapter 9 Motion and Energy

Section 1 Describing Motion 137
Section 2 Speed and Velocity 139
Section 3 Acceleration 142
Section 4 Energy 146

Chapter 10 Forces

Section 1 The Nature of Force 150
Section 2 Friction, Gravity, and Elastic Forces 153
Section 3 Newton's First and Second Laws 157
Section 4 Newton's Third Law 160
Section 5 Rockets and Satellites 164

Chapter 11 Forces in Fluids

Section 1 Pressure 167
Section 2 Floating and Sinking 170
Section 3 Pascal's Principle 174
Section 4 Bernoulli's Principle 177

Unit 4 Astronomy

Chapter 12 Earth, Moon, and Sun

Section 1 Earth in Space 179
Section 2 Gravity and Motion 182
Section 3 Phases, Eclipses, and Tides 185
Section 4 Earth's Moon. 190

Chapter 13 Exploring Space

Section 1 The Science of Rockets. 192
Section 2 The Space Program 196
Section 3 Exploring Space Today 199
Section 4 Using Space Science on Earth. 202

Chapter 14 The Solar System

Section 1 Observing the Solar System 206
Section 2 The Sun 211
Section 3 The Inner Planets 215
Section 4 The Outer Planets 220
Section 5 Comets, Asteroids, and Meteors . . 226
Section 6 Is There Life Beyond Earth? 230

Chapter 15 Stars, Galaxies, and the Universe

Section 1 Telescopes. 232
Section 2 Characteristics of Stars 236
Section 3 Lives of Stars 241
Section 4 Star Systems and Galaxies 245
Section 5 The Expanding Universe 250

Your Keys to Success

How to Read Science

The target reading skills introduced on this page will help you read and understand information in this textbook. Each chapter introduces a reading skill. Developing these reading skills is key to becoming a successful reader in science and other subject areas.

Preview Text Structure By understanding how textbooks are organized, you can gain information from them more effectively. This textbook is organized with red headings and blue subheadings. Before you read, preview the headings. Ask yourself questions to guide you as you read. **(Chapter 1)**

Preview Visuals The visuals in your science textbook provide important information. Visuals are photographs, graphs, tables, diagrams, and illustrations. Before you read, take the time to preview the visuals in a section. Look closely at the title, labels, and captions. Then ask yourself questions about the visuals. **(Chapter 4)**

Sequence Many parts of a science textbook are organized by sequence. Sequence is the order in which a series of events occurs. Some sections may discuss events in a process that has a beginning and an end. Other sections may describe a continuous process that does not have an end. **(Chapters 11 and 12)**

Compare and Contrast Science texts often make comparisons. When you compare and contrast, you examine the similarities and differences between things. You can compare and contrast by using a table or a Venn diagram. **(Chapters 5 and 8)**

Identify Main Ideas As you read, you can understand a section or paragraph more clearly by finding the main idea. The main idea is the most important idea. The details in a section or paragraph support the main idea. Headings and subheadings can often help you identify the main ideas. **(Chapters 2 and 9)**

Identify Supporting Evidence Science textbooks often describe the scientific evidence that supports a theory or hypothesis. Scientific evidence includes data and facts, information whose accuracy can be confirmed by experiments or observation. A hypothesis is a possible explanation for observations made by scientists or an answer to a scientific question. **(Chapter 15)**

Create Outlines You can create outlines to help you clarify the text. An outline shows the relationship between main ideas and supporting details. Use the text structure—headings, subheadings, key concepts, and key terms—to help you figure out information to include in your outline. **(Chapters 3, 7, and 14)**

Take Notes Science chapters are packed with information. Taking good notes is one way to help you remember key ideas and to see the big picture. When you take notes, include key ideas, a few details, and summaries. **(Chapters 6 and 10)**

Target Reading Skills

Each chapter provides a target reading skill with clear instruction to help you read and understand the text. You will apply the skill as you read. Then you will record what you've learned in the section and chapter assessments.

Before You Read
Each chapter introduces a target reading skill and provides examples and practice exercises.

As You Read
As you read, you can use the target reading skill to help you increase your understanding.

After You Read
You can apply the target reading skill in the Section Assessments and in the Chapter Assessments.

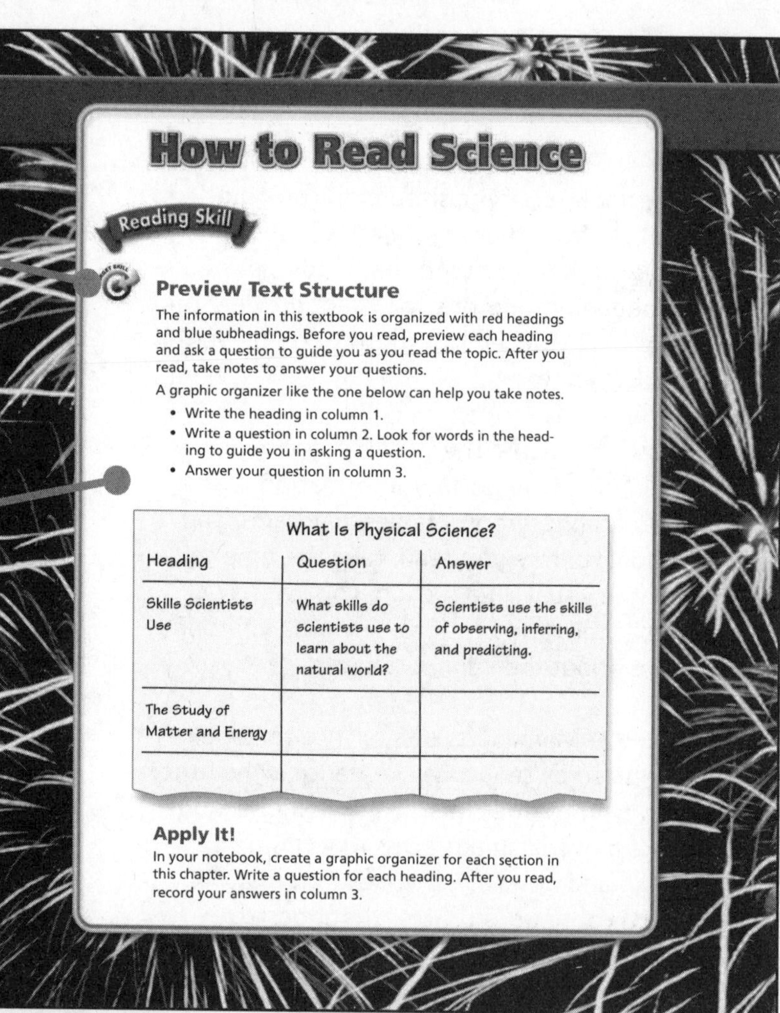

How to Read Science

Reading Skill

Preview Text Structure

The information in this textbook is organized with red headings and blue subheadings. Before you read, preview each heading and ask a question to guide you as you read the topic. After you read, take notes to answer your questions.

A graphic organizer like the one below can help you take notes.

- Write the heading in column 1.
- Write a question in column 2. Look for words in the heading to guide you in asking a question.
- Answer your question in column 3.

What Is Physical Science?

Heading	Question	Answer
Skills Scientists Use	What skills do scientists use to learn about the natural world?	Scientists use the skills of observing, inferring, and predicting.
The Study of Matter and Energy		

Apply It!
In your notebook, create a graphic organizer for each section in this chapter. Write a question for each heading. After you read, record your answers in column 3.

Section 3 Assessment

S 8.8.a, 8.8.b, E-LA: Reading 8.2.0, Math: 7NS1.2

Target Reading Skill Preview Text Structure Complete the graphic organizer for this section. What question did you ask about Weight and Mass? What was your answer?

Reviewing Key Concepts

1. a. **Identifying** What is the standard measurement system used by scientists around the world?
   b. **Predicting** Suppose that two scientists use different measurement systems in their work. What problems might arise if they shared their data?
2. a. **Listing** What are the SI units of length, mass, volume, density, time, and temperature?
   b. **Estimating** Estimate the length of a baseball bat and mass of a baseball in SI units. How can you check how close your estimates are?
   c. **Describing** Outline a step-by-step method for determining the density of a baseball.

Math Practice

Two solid cubes have the same mass. They each have a mass of 50 g.

3. **Calculating Density** Cube A has a volume of 2 cm × 2 cm × 2 cm. What is its density?
4. **Calculating Density** Cube B has a volume of 4 cm × 4 cm × 4 cm. What is its density?

Your Keys to Success

Build Science Vocabulary

Studying science involves learning a new vocabulary. Here are some vocabulary skills to help you learn the meaning of words you do not recognize.

Word Analysis You can use your knowledge of word parts—prefixes, suffixes, and roots—to determine the meaning of unfamiliar words.

Prefixes A prefix is a word part that is added at the beginning of a root or base word to change its meaning. Knowing the meaning of prefixes will help you figure out new words. You will practice this skill in **Chapter 2.**

Suffixes A suffix is a letter or group of letters added to the end of a word to form a new word with a slightly different meaning. Adding a suffix to a word often changes its part of speech. You will practice this skill in **Chapters 3 and 15.**

Word Origins Many science words come to English from other languages, such as Greek and Latin. By learning the meaning of a few common Greek and Latin roots, you can determine the meaning of new science words. You will practice this skill in **Chapters 4, 10, 12, and 14.**

Use Clues to Determine Meaning

When you come across a word you don't recognize in science texts, you can use context clues to figure out what the word means. First look for clues in the word itself. Then look at the surrounding words, sentences, and paragraphs for clues. You will practice this skill in **Chapter 8.**

Identify Multiple Meanings

To understand science concepts, you must use terms precisely. Some familiar words may have different meanings in science. Watch for these multiple-meaning words as you read. You will practice this skill in **Chapters 6 and 11.**

Identify Related Word Forms

You can increase your vocabulary by learning related forms of words or word families. If you know the meaning of a verb form, you may be able to figure out the related noun and adjective forms. You will practice this skill in **Chapter 7.**

atmos +	sphaira =	atmosphere
vapor gas	sphere	a layer of vapor or gases that surrounds Earth

Vocabulary Skills

One of the important steps in reading this science textbook is to be sure that you understand the Key Terms. Your book shows several strategies to help learn important vocabulary.

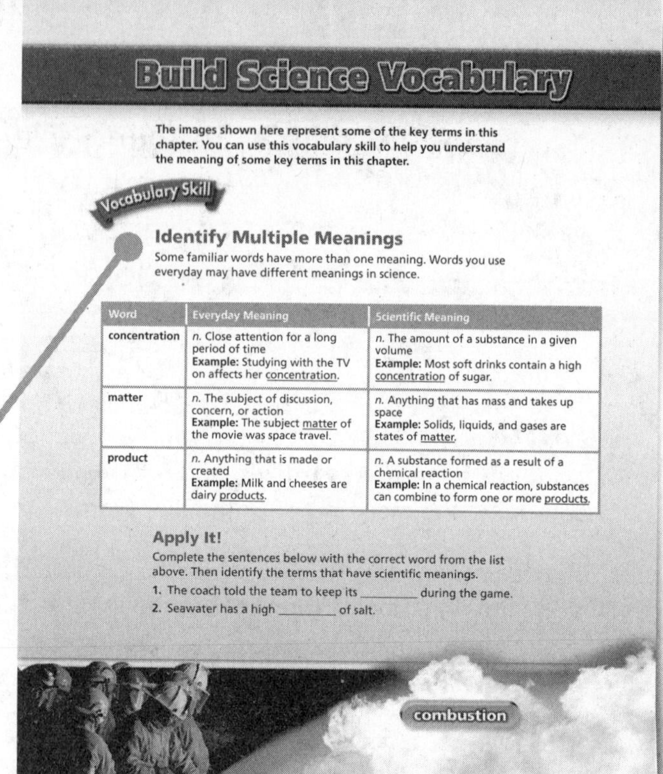

Build Science Vocabulary

The images shown here represent some of the key terms in this chapter. You can use this vocabulary skill to help you understand the meaning of some key terms in this chapter.

Vocabulary Skill

Identify Multiple Meanings

Some familiar words have more than one meaning. Words you use everyday may have different meanings in science.

Word	Everyday Meaning	Scientific Meaning
concentration	*n.* Close attention for a long period of time **Example:** Studying with the TV on affects her concentration.	*n.* The amount of a substance in a given volume **Example:** Most soft drinks contain a high concentration of sugar.
matter	*n.* The subject of discussion, concern, or action **Example:** The subject matter of the movie was space travel.	*n.* Anything that has mass and takes up space **Example:** Solids, liquids, and gases are states of matter.
product	*n.* Anything that is made or created **Example:** Milk and cheeses are dairy products.	*n.* A substance formed as a result of a chemical reaction **Example:** In a chemical reaction, substances can combine to form one or more products.

Apply It!

Complete the sentences below with the correct word from the list above. Then identify the terms that have scientific meanings.

1. The coach told the team to keep its _______ during the game.
2. Seawater has a high _______ of salt.

Before You Read

Each chapter introduces a Vocabulary Skill with examples and practice exercises. Key Terms come alive through visuals. The beginning of each section lists the Key Terms.

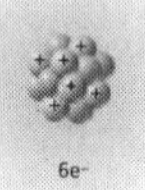

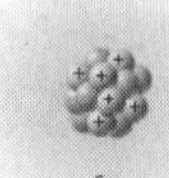

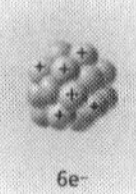

6e⁻ — **Carbon-12** 6 Neutrons

6e⁻ — **Carbon-13** 7 Neutrons

6e⁻ — **Carbon-14** 8 Neutrons

FIGURE 10
Isotopes
Atoms of all isotopes of carbon contain 6 protons and 6 electrons, but they differ in their number of neutrons. Carbon-12 is the most common isotope.
Interpreting Diagrams *Which isotope of carbon has the largest mass number?*

Isotopes and Mass Number Although the number of protons is fixed for a particular element, the same is not true for the number of neutrons in the nucleus. Atoms of the same element that have different numbers of neutrons are called **isotopes** (EYE suh tohps). Three carbon isotopes are illustrated in Figure 10. Each carbon atom has 6 protons and 6 electrons. But the number of neutrons is 6, 7, or 8. An isotope is identified by its **mass number,** which is the sum of the protons and neutrons in the nucleus of an atom. The most common isotope of carbon has a mass number of 12 (6 protons + 6 neutrons), and may be written as "carbon-12." Two other isotopes are carbon-13 and carbon-14. Despite their different mass numbers, all three carbon isotopes react the same way chemically.

Hydrogen also has three isotopes. All hydrogen atoms have one proton in the nucleus. The most common isotope is hydrogen-1 (1 proton + 0 neutrons). The others are hydrogen-2 (1 proton + 1 neutron) and hydrogen-3 (1 proton + 2 neutrons). Hydrogen-2 is called deuterium. Hydrogen-3 is called tritium.

As You Read

Each Key Term is highlighted in yellow, appears in boldfaced type, and is followed by a definition.

Section 1 Assessment

S 8.3.a, 8.7.b, E-LA: Reading 8.1.2

Vocabulary Skill Greek Word Origins Use what you know about the Greek word *atomos* to explain the meaning of *atom*.

Reviewing Key Concepts

1. a. Reviewing Why did atomic theory change with time?
   b. Describing Describe Bohr's model of the atom. What specific information did Bohr contribute to scientists' understanding of the atom?
   c. Comparing and Contrasting How is the modern atomic model different from Bohr's model?
2. a. Reviewing What are the three main particles in the modern model of an atom?
   b. Explaining What is atomic number? How is it used to distinguish one element from another?
   c. Applying Concepts The atomic number of nitrogen is 7. How many protons, neutrons, and electrons make up an atom of nitrogen-15?

Lab zone At-Home Activity

Modeling Atoms Build a three-dimensional model of an atom using materials such as beads, cotton, and clay. Show the model to your family, and explain what makes atoms of different elements different from one another.

130 ♦

After You Read

You can practice the Vocabulary Skill in the Section Assessments. You can apply your understanding of the Key Terms in the Chapter Assessments.

Your Keys to Success

Build Science Vocabulary

High-Use Academic Words

High-use academic words are words that are used frequently in classroom reading, writing, and discussions. They are different from Key Terms because they appear in many subject areas.

Learn the Words

Each unit contains a chapter that introduces high-use academic words. The introduction provides parts of speech, definitions, example sentences, and practice excercises introduces a target reading skill and provides examples and practice exercises.

Practice Using the Words

You can practice using the high-use academic words in the section assessments.

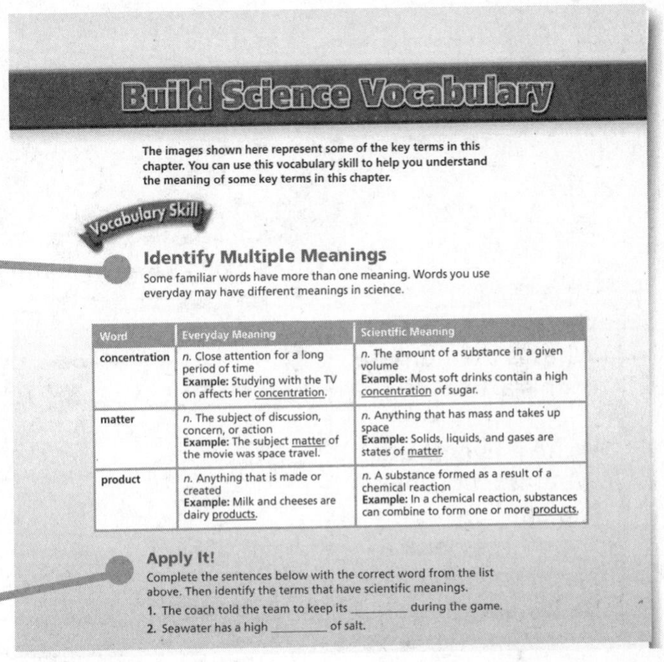

Build Science Vocabulary

The images shown here represent some of the key terms in this chapter. You can use this vocabulary skill to help you understand the meaning of some key terms in this chapter.

Vocabulary Skill

Identify Multiple Meanings

Some familiar words have more than one meaning. Words you use everyday may have different meanings in science.

Word	Everyday Meaning	Scientific Meaning
concentration	*n.* Close attention for a long period of time **Example:** Studying with the TV on affects her concentration.	*n.* The amount of a substance in a given volume **Example:** Most soft drinks contain a high concentration of sugar.
matter	*n.* The subject of discussion, concern, or action **Example:** The subject matter of the movie was space travel.	*n.* Anything that has mass and takes up space **Example:** Solids, liquids, and gases are states of matter.
product	*n.* Anything that is made or created **Example:** Milk and cheeses are dairy products.	*n.* A substance formed as a result of a chemical reaction **Example:** In a chemical reaction, substances can combine to form one or more products.

Apply It!

Complete the sentences below with the correct word from the list above. Then identify the terms that have scientific meanings.

1. The coach told the team to keep its ________ during the game.
2. Seawater has a high ________ of salt.

Focus on Physical Science High-Use Academic Words

Learning the meaning of these words will help you improve your reading comprehension in all subject areas.

alter	contribute	factor	occur	remove
area	convert	feature	percent	resource
category	convert	feature	physical	reverse
channel	define	function	positive	series
concept	detect	generate	predictable	source
conduct	distinct	indicate	principle	structure
constant	diversity	individual	process	sustain
construct	enable	interpret	process	technique
consumer	environment	layer	proportion	theory
contact	estimate	major	range	transfer
contract	expand	method	region	trigger
contrast	exposure	obtain	reject	uniform
			release	vary

Investigations

You can explore the concepts in this textbook through inquiry. Like a real scientist, you can develop your own scientific questions and perform labs and activities to find answers. Follow the steps below when doing a lab.

1 **Read the whole lab.**

2 **Write a purpose.** What is the purpose of this activity?

3 **Write a hypothesis.** What is a possible explanation? Hypotheses lead to predictions that can be tested.

4 **Follow each step in the procedure.** Pay attention to safety icons.

5 **Record your data.**

6 **Analyze your results.** Answering the questions will help you draw conclusions.

7 **Communicate your results in a written report or oral presentation.** Your report should include:

- a hypothesis
- a purpose
- the steps of the procedure
- a record of your results
- a conclusion

Oral presentations should include all of the information that you would include in a lab report.

Lab zone **Skills Lab**

Making Sense of Density

S 8.8.b, 8.9.b

Problem

Does the density of a material vary with volume?

Skills Focus

drawing conclusions, measuring, controlling variables

Materials

- balance
- water
- paper towels
- metric ruler
- graduated cylinder, 100-mL
- wooden stick, about 6 cm long
- ball of modeling clay, about 5 cm wide
- crayon with paper removed

Procedure

1. Use a balance to find the mass of the wooden stick. Record the mass in a data table like the one shown above right.
2. Add enough water to a graduated cylinder so that the stick can be completely submerged. Measure the initial volume of the water.
3. Place the stick in the graduated cylinder. Measure the new volume of the water.
4. The volume of the stick is the difference between the water levels in Steps 2 and 3. Calculate this volume and record it.
5. The density of the stick equals its mass divided by its volume. Calculate and record its density.
6. Thoroughly dry the stick with a paper towel. Then carefully break the stick into two pieces. Repeat Steps 1 through 5 with one piece. Then, repeat Steps 1 through 5 with the other piece.
7. Repeat Steps 1 through 6 using the clay rolled into a rope.
8. Repeat using the crayon.

Data Table

Object	Mass (g)	Volume Change (cm^3)	Density (g/cm^3)
Wooden stick			
Whole			
Piece 1			
Piece 2			
Modeling clay			
Whole			
Piece 1			
Piece 2			
Crayon			
Whole			
Piece 1			
Piece 2			

Analyze and Conclude

1. **Measuring** For each object you tested, compare the density of the whole object with the densities of the pieces of the object.
2. **Drawing Conclusions** Use your results to explain how density can be used to identify a material.
3. **Controlling Variables** Why did you dry the objects in Step 6?
4. **Communicating** Write a paragraph explaining how you would change the procedure to obtain more data. Tell how having more data would affect your answers to Questions 1 and 2 above.

Design an Experiment

Design an experiment you could use to determine the density of olive oil. With your teacher's permission, carry out your plan. Use the library or the Internet to find the actual density of olive oil. Compare your experimental value with the actual value, and explain why they may differ.

Lab Report

Purpose: To determine how the density of a material varies with volume.

Hypothesis:

For more information on Science Inquiry, Scientific Investigations and Safety refer to the Skills Handbook and Appendix A.

What Is Physical Science? (pages 6–9)

Skills Scientists Use (pages 7–8)

Key Concept: **Scientists use the skills of observing, inferring, and predicting to learn more about the natural world.**

- **Science** is a way of learning about the natural world by gathering information.
- **Observing** means using your senses to gather information. You can make either qualitative observations or quantitative observations.
- **Qualitative observations** deal with descriptions that do not include numbers.
- **Quantitative observations** deal with numbers—the amount of something.
- **Inferring** is explaining or interpreting the things you observe. When you infer, you make an inference.
- **Predicting** means making a forecast of what will happen in the future. You make a prediction based either on what you have experienced in the past or on current evidence.

Answer the following questions. Use your textbook and the ideas above.

1. Circle the letter of each item that you would base a prediction on.
   - **a.** evidence that you have recently collected
   - **b.** a feeling about what will happen
   - **c.** your experience in the past

2. Draw a line from each term to its meaning.

Term	**Meaning**
science	**a.** observations that deal with numbers
observing	**b.** explaining or interpreting the things you observe
quantitative observations	**c.** using your senses to gather information
qualitative observations	**d.** a way of learning about the natural world
inferring	**e.** making a forecast of what will happen in the future
predicting	**f.** observations that deal with descriptions that do not include numbers

3. The picture below shows a spider called a tarantula. Circle the letter of a quantitative observation about this animal.

a. A tarantula is scary.

b. A tarantula has eight legs.

c. A tarantula eats insects.

The Study of Matter and Energy (pages 8–9)

Key Concept: **Physical science is the study of matter, energy, and the changes they undergo.**

- Physical science is divided into two main areas: chemistry and physics.
- **Chemistry** is the study of the properties of matter. It also is the study of how matter changes.
- **Physics** is the study of matter and energy. It is also the study of how matter and energy interact. Topics in physics include motion, forces, forms of energy, and laws about energy.

Answer the following questions. Use your textbook and the ideas above.

4. Read each word in the box. In each sentence below, fill in one of the words.

chemistry	biology	physics

a. The study of matter and energy is called ____________________.

b. The study of the properties of matter and how matter changes is called ____________________.

5. Circle the letter of each topic that is included in physics.

a. forms of energy

b. motion

c. how matter changes

Scientific Inquiry (pages 10–15)

The Process of Inquiry (pages 10–14)

Key Concept: **The processes that scientists use in inquiry include posing questions, developing hypotheses, designing experiments, collecting and interpreting data, drawing conclusions, and communicating ideas and results.**

- **Scientific inquiry** refers to the different ways scientists study the natural world.
- Not all questions are scientific. Scientific questions are questions that you can answer by making observations. Scientific inquiry cannot answer questions based on opinions, values, or judgments.
- To answer a scientific question, a scientist develops a hypothesis. A **hypothesis** (plural: *hypotheses*) is a possible explanation or answer to a scientific question.
- Scientists can test a hypothesis by designing an experiment. They begin to plan their experiment by first looking at all the parameters. A **parameter** is a factor that can be measured in an experiment.
- In a scientific experiment, only one variable parameter is changed on purpose. The variable that is changed on purpose is called the **manipulated variable**. By changing the manipulated variable, another factor may change in response. The factor that may change in response to the manipulated variable is called the **responding variable**.
- **Data** are facts, figures, and other evidence that a scientist gathers by observation. Data can be organized in a table called a data table.

Answer the following questions. Use your textbook and the ideas on page 14.

1. The different ways scientists study the natural world is called scientific ____________________ .

2. Circle the letter of each scientific question.
   a. Why doesn't my CD player work?
   b. What is the best song on this CD?
   c. How long will this CD play?

3. Draw a line from each term to its meaning.

Term	**Meaning**
hypothesis	**a.** a factor that can be measured in an experiment
parameter	**b.** facts, figures, and other evidence that a scientist gathers by observation
data	**c.** a possible explanation or answer to a scientific question

4. Read each word in the box. In each sentence below, fill in correct word.

manipulated	experimental	responding

   a. The variable that is changed on purpose in an experiment is called the ____________________ variable.
   b. The factor that may change in response to the manipulated variable is called the ____________________ variable.

5. Is the following sentence true or false? A testable hypothesis is one that can be proved or disproved by experiment or observation. __________

6. The diagram below is a model of the scientific inquiry process. Circle the step in the process where a scientist can test a hypothesis.

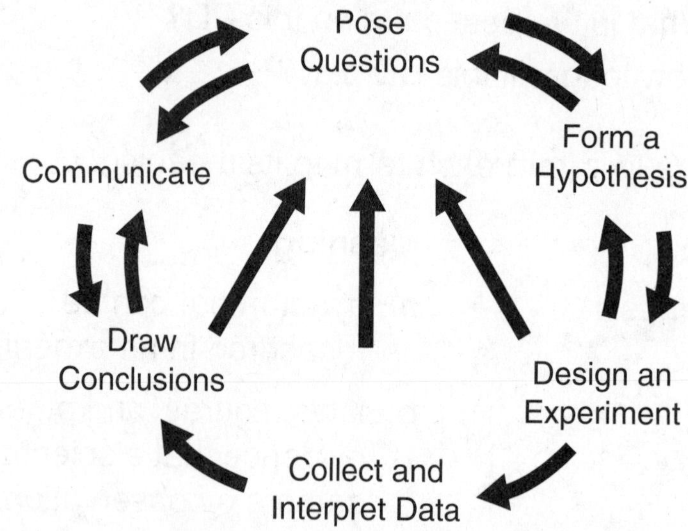

How Science Develops (pages 14–15)

***Key Concept:* Scientists use models and develop theories and laws to increase people's understanding of the natural world.**

- When a scientist cannot observe an object or a process, the scientist may make a model. A model might be a picture, a diagram, a computer image, or even a mathematical equation. A model represents—stands for—a real object or process.
- Certain models may look like the real thing. An example is a drawing of the solar system. Other models, such as a mathematical equation, are not meant to look like the real thing.

- A **scientific theory** is an explanation for a wide range of observations or experimental results. For example, the atomic theory says that all substances are made up of tiny particles called atoms.
- Scientists accept a scientific theory only when there is a lot of evidence that supports the theory.
- A **scientific law** is a statement that describes what scientists expect to happen every time certain conditions exist. For example, according to the law of gravity, when you drop a pencil, it will fall to the floor.

Answer the following questions. Use your textbook and the ideas on page 16 and above.

7. Is the following sentence true or false? A model always looks like a real object. __________

8. Read each word in the box. In each sentence below, fill in one of the words.

law	hypothesis	theory

a. An explanation for a wide range of observations or experimental results is a scientific ____________________.

b. A statement that describes what scientists expect will happen every time certain conditions exist is a scientific ____________________.

Measurement (pages 16–26)

A Standard Measurement System (page 17)

Key Concept: **Using SI as the standard system of measurement allows scientists to compare data and communicate with each other about their results.**

- The **metric system** is a system of measurement based on the number 10.
- Scientists use a version of the metric system called the International System of Units. Scientists call this metric system **SI**.
- Each SI unit is ten times larger than the next smallest unit. Each SI unit is one tenth the size of the next largest unit.

Answer the following questions. Use your textbook and the ideas above.

1. Read each word in the box. In each sentence below, fill in the correct word or words.

metric system	SI	measurement system

a. The ____________________ is a system of measurement based on the number 10.

b. Scientists call the International System of Units ____________________.

2. Is the following sentence true or false? Each SI unit is ten times larger than the next smallest unit. __________

Length (pages 18–20)

***Key Concept:* The basic unit of length in SI is the meter (m).**

- Length is the distance from one point to another.
- One meter is about the distance from the floor to a doorknob.
- 1 meter = 100 centimeters
- 1 meter = 1,000 millimeters
- 1,000 meters = 1 kilometer
- A common tool to measure length is the metric ruler. A metric ruler is divided into centimeters and millimeters.

Answer the following questions. Use your textbook and the ideas above.

3. The basic SI unit of length is the ______________________.

4. 1 meter = ______________________ millimeters

Weight and Mass (pages 20–21)

***Key Concept:* The SI unit of mass is the kilogram (kg).**

- **Mass** is how much matter there is in an object.
- A wooden baseball bat is about 1 kilogram.
- 1 gram = 1,000 milligrams
- 1 kilogram = 1,000 grams
- A common tool to measure mass is the triple-beam balance. You place the object you want to measure on the pan of the balance.
- Weight is not the same thing as mass. **Weight** is a measure of the force of gravity acting on an object.

Answer the following questions. Use your textbook and the ideas on page 19.

5. Draw a line from each term to its meaning.

Term	**Meaning**
mass	**a.** a measure of the force of gravity acting on an object
weight	**b.** a measure of how much matter there is in an object

6. The picture below shows a triple-beam balance. Draw an X where you would place an object on the balance to find its mass.

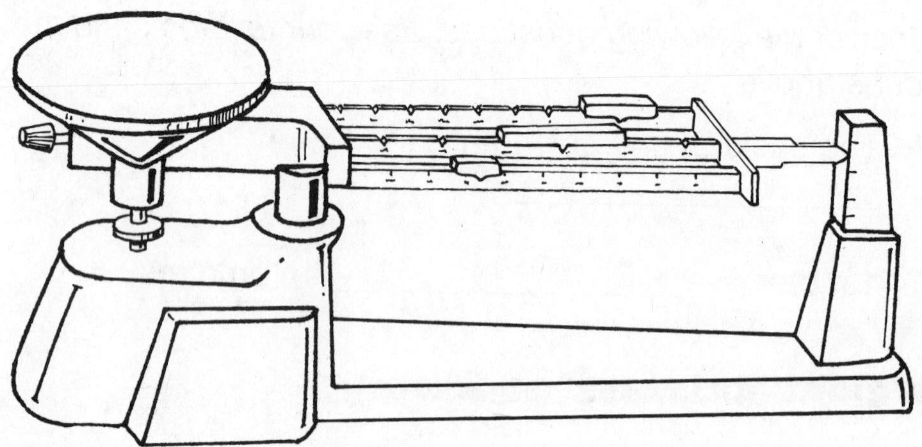

Volume (pages 20–23)

Key Concept: **The SI unit of volume is the cubic meter (m^3).**

- **Volume** is the amount of space an object takes up. Scientists use a unit known as the liter (L) to measure the volume of a liquid.

- Scientists commonly use a graduated cylinder to measure liquid volumes. The top surface of water in a graduated cylinder is curved. The curve is called the **meniscus**. To measure the volume of water in a graduated cylinder, you read the millimeter marking at the bottom of the curve.
- 1 liter = 1,000 milliliters
- You can calculate the volume of a regular solid using this formula:

$$\text{Volume} = \text{Length} \times \text{Width} \times \text{Height}$$

- Scientists use the cubic centimeter (cm^3) or the cubic meter (m^3) when measuring the volume of a rectangular solid.
- To measure a rock or some other object with an irregular shape, you place the object in water and measure how much the water level rises.

Answer the following questions. Use your textbook and the ideas on page 20 and above.

7. The amount of space an object takes up is called

______________________.

8. The picture below shows water in a graduated cylinder. Draw a line at the place where you would read how many millimeters of water there are in the cylinder.

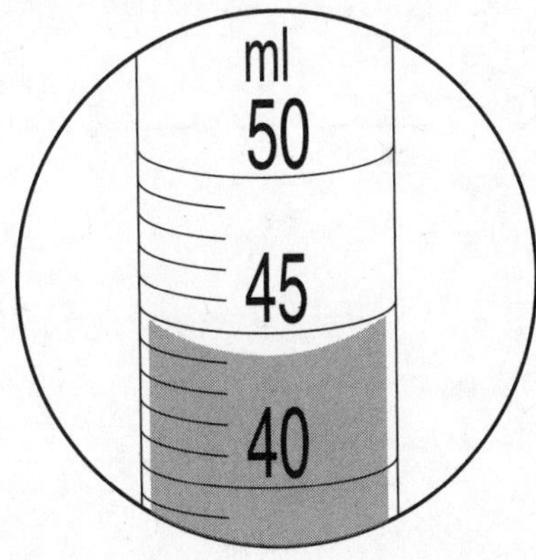

Density (pages 24–25)

***Key Concept:* The SI unit of density is the kilogram per cubic meter (kg/m^3).**

- **Density** is how much mass there is in a given volume.
- The formula to calculate density is:

$$\text{Density} = \frac{\text{Mass}}{\text{Volume}}$$

- There are two common units of density: grams per cubic centimeter (g/cm^3) and grams per milliliter (g/mL).
- An object will float if it is less dense than the surrounding liquid.
- The density of water is 1 g/cm^3. A piece of wood that is less dense than water will float. A piece of metal that is denser than water will sink.

Answer the following questions. Use your textbook and the ideas above.

9. Density is how much ____________________ there is in a given volume.

10. Suppose a metal object has a mass of 60 g and a volume of 30 cm^3. What is the object's density? Use the formula given above. Show your calculations in the space below.

Density = ____________________

Time (page 25)

Key Concept: **The second (s) is the SI unit of time.**

- Your heart beats about once per second.
- 1 second = 1,000 milliseconds
- There are 60 seconds in a minute. There are 60 minutes in an hour.
- Clocks and watches are used to measure time.

Answer the following question. Use your textbook and the ideas above.

11. The SI unit used to measure time is the

______________________.

Temperature (page 26)

Key Concept: **The kelvin (K) is the SI unit of temperature.**

- Scientists commonly use the Celsius temperature scale. On the Celsius scale, water freezes at 0°C and boils at 100°C.
- Scientists also use the Kelvin scale to measure temperature. On the Kelvin scale, water freezes at 273 K, and water boils at 373 K.
- Absolute zero is the coldest possible temperature on any scale. Absolute zero is equal to −273°C on the Celsius scale. Absolute zero is equal to 0 K on the Kelvin scale.
- You can measure temperature with a thermometer.

Answer the following questions. Use your textbook and the ideas on page 23.

12. The official SI unit for temperature is the ______________________.

13. Circle the letter of the temperature at which water freezes on the Celsius scale.

a. 0°C

b. 32°C

c. 100°C

Mathematics and Science (pages 30–33)

Estimation (page 30)

***Key Concept:* Scientists must sometimes rely on estimates when they cannot obtain exact numbers.**

- An **estimate** is an idea of what a number is when you do not know exactly what the number is.
- An estimate is not a guess. An estimate is based on information that you know.
- For example, a park ranger might estimate how many trees are in a forest. The ranger's estimate might be based on counting the trees in a small area. The ranger would then use that number to make an estimate of how many trees are in the whole forest.

Answer the following questions. Use your textbook and the ideas above.

1. An idea of what a number is when you do not know exactly what the number is a(an)

______________________.

2. Is the following sentence true or false? An estimate is a guess. __________

Accuracy and Reproducibility (page 31)

***Key Concept:* Scientists aim for both accuracy and reproducibility in their measurements.**

- **Accuracy** is how close a measurement is to the true value. For example, suppose you measure a paper clip to be 1 gram, and its true value is 1 gram. In that case, your measurement is accurate.

- **Reproducibility** is how close a group of measurements are to each other. For example, suppose you measure the mass of a paper clip 10 times. If you measure close to the same mass each time, your measurements are reproducible.
- You need to make sure that a measurement is both accurate and reproducible:
  1. To make a measurement accurate, you should use good measuring tool. You also need to measure carefully.
  2. To make your measurement reproducible, you need to repeat the measurement a few times.

Answer the following questions. Use your textbook and the ideas on page 25 and above.

3. Read each word in the box. In each sentence below, fill in one of the words.

reproducibility	accuracy	estimation

a. How close a measurement is to the true value is ____________________.

b. How close a group of measurements are to each other is ____________________.

4. Circle the letter of each sentence that is true about accuracy and reproducibility.

a. To make your measurement reproducible, you need to repeat the measurement a few times.

b. To make a measurement accurate, you should use a good measuring tool.

c. Only accuracy is important when you make measurements.

5. The picture above shows four darts that were thrown into a dart board. Circle the letter of which sentence describes the four throws together.

a. The throws were neither accurate nor reproducible.

b. The throws were accurate but not reproducible.

c. The throws were both accurate and reproducible.

Significant Figures and Precision (pages 32–33)

Key Concept: **Scientists use significant figures to express precision in their measurements and calculations.**

- **Significant figures** refer to the digits—the individual numbers—in a measurement. For example, suppose a measurement is 5.3 cm. There are two digits in this measurement.
- When you measure something, you give significance, or importance, to each digit in the measurement. In a measurement, all the digits that you have measured exactly are significant figures. In addition, the last digit on the right is a significant figure. That last digit is an estimate.

- When you add or subtract measurement, the answer can have only as many figures after the decimal point as the measurement with the fewest figures after the decimal point.
- When you multiply or divide measurements, the answer can have only the same number of significant figures as the measurement with the fewest significant figures.

Answer the following questions. Use your textbook and the ideas on page 27 and above.

6. Circle the letter of each description that the significant digits in a measurement include.

  a. all of the digits that have been measured exactly

  b. two digits whose values have been estimated

  c. one digit whose value has been estimated

7. A scientist makes two measurements on a field. The first is 6.3 m. The second is 22.42 m. What is the total length of the two measurements? Do your calculations in the space below. Make sure your answer has the correct number of significant figures.

Total length = ____________________

Graphs in Science (pages 34–41)

The Importance of Graphs (pages 35–39)

***Key Concept:* Line graphs are used to display data to show how one variable (the responding variable) changes in response to another variable (the manipulated variable).**

- A **graph** is a "picture" of the data.
- There are three main types of graphs: line graphs, bar graphs, and circle graphs.
- A line graph can show clearly how the responding variable changes in response to changes in the manipulated variable.
- The **horizontal axis** of a line graph runs left to right. It is also called the *x* axis. You label the horizontal axis with the name of the manipulated variable.
- The **vertical axis** of a line graph runs up and down. It is also called the *y* axis. You label the vertical axis with the name of the responding variable.
- The point where the two axes meet is called the **origin** of the graph.
- A **coordinate** is a pair of numbers used to find the position of a point on the graph.
- A **data point** is the point where an imaginary line from the horizontal axis crosses with an imaginary line from the vertical axis.
- A **linear graph** is a line graph that has a straight line when you plot all the data points.

Answer the following questions. Use your textbook and the ideas above.

1. A "picture" of data is a(an) ____________________.

2. The picture below shows the two axes of a line graph. Write an "H" on the horizontal axis. Write a "V" on the vertical axis.

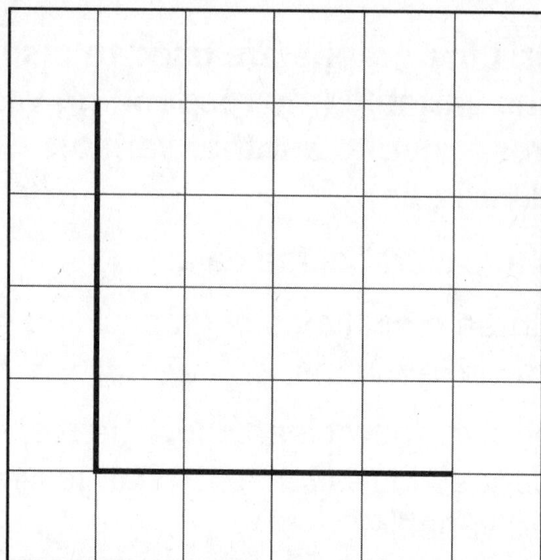

3. Draw a line from each term to its description.

Term	Description
data point	**a.** the point where the two axes meet
coordinate	**b.** the point where an imaginary line from the horizontal axis crosses with an imaginary line from the vertical axis
origin	**c.** a pair of numbers used to find the position of a point on the graph

4. A line graph that has a straight line when you plot all the data points is called a(an) ______________________ graph.

5. Circle the letter of each sentence that is true about line graphs.

a. The vertical axis is also called the *x* axis.

b. You label the horizontal axis with the name of the manipulated variable.

c. Line graphs are used to display data.

Why Draw a Line of Best Fit? (page 38)

***Key Concept:* A line of best fit emphasizes the overall trend shown by all the data taken as a whole.**

- A **line of best fit** is a smooth line that shows the main pattern of a graph. There may be data points that are not on the line of best fit.
- You cannot simply connect the data points to create a line graph. If the data points seem to follow along a straight line, draw a straight line.
- When you draw a line of best fit, include as many data points as possible on the line.
- When you draw a line of best fit, try to have the same number of points above the line as below the line.

Answer the following questions. Use your textbook and the ideas above.

6. A smooth line that shows the main pattern of the graph is called a line of ____________________.

7. Is the following sentence true or false? A line of best fit is a smooth line that shows the main pattern of a graph.

____

Slope (page 39)

Key Concept: **The slope of a graph line tells you how much *y* changes for every change in *x*.**

- **Slope** is how steep the graph line is.
- Two data points on the line will give you two pairs of numbers, such as: (3, 5) and (6, 10). The *x* number in the first pair—3—is called X_1. The *x* number in the second pair—6—is called X_2. The *y* number in the first pair—5—is called Y_1. The *y* number in the second pair—10—is called Y_2.
- To calculate slope, first find the "rise" with this formula:

$$\text{Rise} = Y_2 - Y_1$$

- Next, find the "run" with this formula:

$$\text{Run} = X_2 - X_1$$

- Once you have found the rise and the run, use this formula:

$$\text{Slope} = \frac{\text{Rise}}{\text{Run}}$$

Answer the following questions. Use your textbook and the ideas above.

8. The steepness of a graph line is called its

______________________.

9. Two points on a graph line have the coordinates (10, 5) and (20, 10). What is the slope of the line? Use the formula above. Show calculations in the space below.

Slope = ______________________

Using Graphs to Identify Trends (pages 40–41)

***Key Concept:* Line graphs are powerful tools in science because they allow you to identify trends and make predictions.**

- By looking at a linear graph, you can make predictions.
- A line graph that does not have a straight line is called a **nonlinear graph**. By looking at a nonlinear graph, you can sometimes see patterns. From these patterns, you can make predictions. For example, a graph may show a repeating pattern.
- Some nonlinear graphs show no pattern. In that case, there is no trend in the data.

Answer the following questions. Use your textbook and the ideas above.

10. A line graph that does not have a straight line is called a(an) ______________________ graph.

11. The graph below is a nonlinear graph. Circle the letter of the sentence that describes the graph's trend.

a. The number of bacterial cells increases sharply.

b. The number of bacterial cells stays the same.

c. The number of bacterial cells decreases sharply.

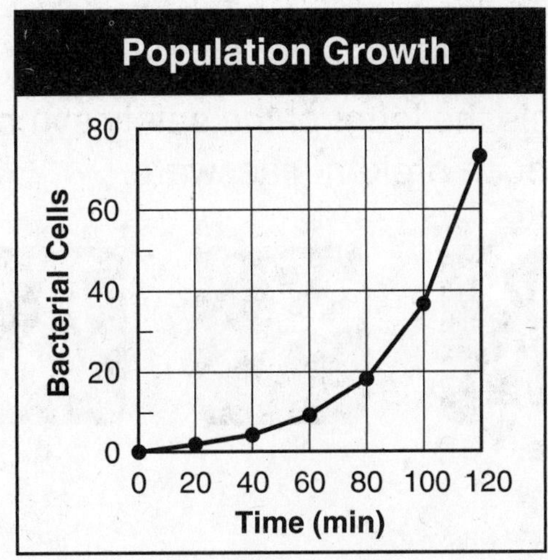

Science Laboratory Safety (pages 43–47)

Safety in the Lab (pages 44–46)

Key Concept: **Good preparation helps you stay safe when doing science activities in the laboratory.**

- To prepare for work in a science laboratory, you must know how to use the equipment. Lab equipment might include a thermometer, balance, or graduated cylinder.
- You should begin preparing the day before the lab. Make sure you understand all the directions. Read the safety guidelines for any equipment you will be using.
- When performing a lab, the most important safety rule is: Always follow your teacher's instructions and the textbook directions exactly.
- Make sure you are familiar with all the safety symbols.

Answer the following questions. Use your textbook and the ideas above.

1. Circle the letter of when you should start preparing for a lab.
   - **a.** the day before the lab
   - **b.** an hour before the lab
   - **c.** when the lab begins

2. Each of the pictures below is a laboratory safety symbol. Circle the letter of the safety symbol that warns you not to touch broken glassware.

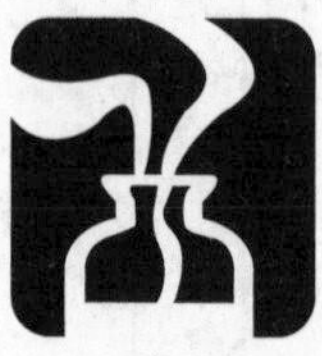
a.

b.

c.

Safety in the Field (page 46)

***Key Concept:* Just as in the laboratory, good preparation helps you stay safe when doing science activities in the field.**

- The "field" includes any area outdoors. You are doing work in the field when you do science in the schoolyard or at a park, beach, or any other place outside.
- You may have safety problems in the field. For example, you might have bad weather or touch poison ivy.
- Whenever you do field work, first tell an adult when and where you are going.
- Never do a field investigation alone.

Answer the following questions. Use your textbook and the ideas above.

3. Circle the letter of each place where you could do an investigation in the field.

- **a.** the school parking lot
- **b.** the classroom laboratory
- **c.** the local park

4. Is the following sentence true or false? You should never do a field investigation alone. __________

In Case of an Accident (page 47)

***Key Concept:* When any accident occurs, no matter how minor, notify your teacher immediately. Then, listen to your teacher's directions and carry them out quickly.**

- Tell your teacher right away if there is an accident.

- Make sure you know where emergency equipment is in your lab room. Learn how to use the emergency equipment.
- Know what to do if you burn yourself, cut yourself, spill something on your skin, or put something in your eye. For example, if you spill something on your skin, you and your teacher should pour large amounts of water on your skin.

Answer the following questions. Use your textbook and the ideas on page 35 and above.

5. Circle the letter of what you should do immediately if an accident occurs in the laboratory.

a. Find emergency equipment.

b. Ask another student what to do.

c. Tell your teacher.

6. Is the following sentence true or false? Only the teacher needs to know where emergency equipment is in the laboratory. __________

Describing Matter (pages 58–67)

Properties of Matter (pages 59–61)

Key Concept: **Every form of matter has two kinds of properties—physical properties and chemical properties.**

- **Matter** is anything that has mass and takes up space. All the "stuff" around you is matter. Your pencil is matter. Water is matter. Air is matter, too.
- A **physical property** is how matter looks, feels, smells, sounds, and tastes. One physical property of water is that it is a liquid at room temperature. Other physical properties are color, hardness, and being able to stick to magnets.
- A **chemical property** tells how matter can change into new kinds of matter. For example, being able to catch fire and burn is a chemical property of wood. Another chemical property is being able to rust.

Answer the following questions. Use your textbook and the ideas above.

1. Anything that has mass and takes up space is

a. matter.

b. a physical property.

c. a chemical property.

Name ______________________ Date ________________ Class __________

2. Complete the table below. Decide if each property of matter is a physical property or a chemical property. Write *P* if it is a physical property. Write *C* if it is a chemical property.

Properties of Matter	
Property	**Physical Property or Chemical Property?**
Rusting	**a.**
Color	**b.**
Burning	**c.**
Hardness	**d.**

Elements (pages 62–63)

***Key Concept:* Elements are the simplest substances.**

- An **element** is a kind of matter that cannot be broken down into any other kind of substance. Gold is an element. Iron and oxygen are elements, too.
- Every element has different physical properties. Every element also has different chemical properties.
- An **atom** is the smallest part of an element. Each element is made up of only one kind of atom. The atoms of gold are different from the atoms of iron.
- Most atoms can join with other atoms. Joining forms a **chemical bond,** which is a pulling force that holds atoms together.

Answer the following questions. Use your textbook and the ideas on page 38.

3. Read each word in the box. In each sentence below, fill in one of the words.

molecule	element	atom

a. The smallest part of an element is a(an)

____________________.

b. A substance that cannot be broken down into any other kind of substance is called a(an)

____________________.

4. A pulling force that holds atoms together is called a

a. substance.

b. chemical bond.

c. chemical property.

Compounds (page 64)

***Key Concept:* When elements are chemically combined, they form compounds having properties that are different from those of the uncombined elements.**

- **Compounds** are made up of the atoms of two or more elements joined together. The joined atoms are held together by chemical bonds.
- When elements combine, their physical properties and chemical properties change. A compound has properties different from each element it is made of.

Answer the following questions. Use your textbook and the ideas on page 39.

5. The picture shows a model of a carbon atom and an oxygen atom. The picture also shows a compound formed when an atom of carbon joins with an atom of oxygen. Circle the letter of the compound.

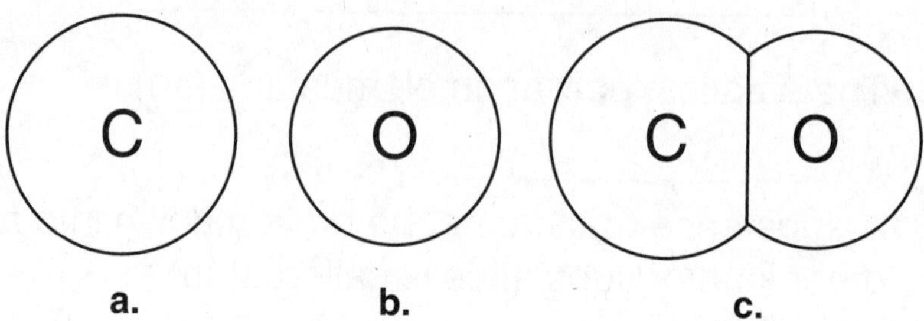

6. Circle the letter of each sentence that is true about elements in compounds.

a. When elements combine, their properties stay the same.

b. When elements combine, their properties change.

c. When elements combine, they have no properties.

Mixtures (pages 65–67)

Key Concept: **Each substance in a mixture keeps its individual properties. Also, the parts of a mixture are not combined in a set ratio.**

- A **mixture** is made up of two or more compounds or elements that are together in the same place.
- A mixture is different from a compound in two ways:
  1. The parts of a mixture are not chemically combined.
  2. The properties of each part of a mixture do not change when the parts are mixed together. For example, when you mix sugar into water, you can still taste the sugar.

- A **solution** is one kind of mixture. In a solution, the parts are very evenly mixed together. A mixture of sugar and water is a solution.
- In other mixtures, you can see the different parts. For example, you can see the lettuce, tomatoes, and olives in a salad.
- A mixture is easy to separate into its different parts because the parts keep their properties. For example, you can pick the olives out of a salad.

Answer the following questions. Use your textbook and the ideas on page 40 and above.

7. Read each word in the box. In each sentence below, fill in one of the words.

mixture	molecule	solution

a. A kind of mixture in which the different parts are very evenly mixed is called a

____________________.

b. Two or more compounds or elements together in the same place is called a

____________________.

8. Is the following sentence true or false? Each part of a mixture keeps its properties. __________

Changes in Matter (pages 68–72)

Physical Change (page 69)

***Key Concept:* A substance that undergoes a physical change is still the same substance after the change.**

- A **physical change** changes the way matter looks. It does not change the matter into a new kind of matter.
- Melting ice to form liquid water is a physical change. Dissolving sugar in water is another physical change. Bending a paperclip is also a physical change.

Answer the following questions. Use your textbook and the ideas above.

1. Is the following sentence true or false? A physical change changes matter into a new kind of matter.

   ____

2. Use the words in the box to complete the concept map about physical change.

Burning	Bending	Dissolving

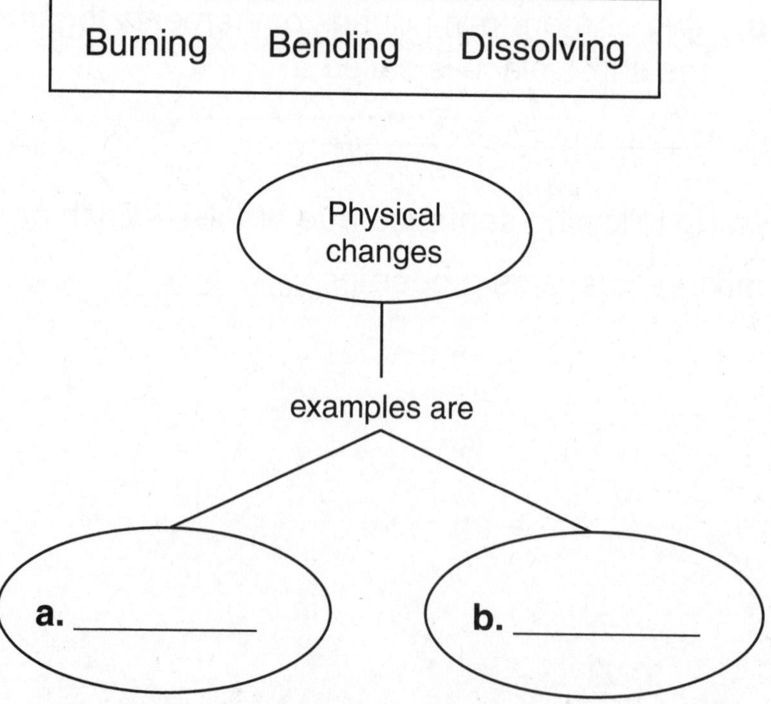

Chemical Change (pages 70–71)

***Key Concept:* Unlike a physical change, a chemical change produces new substances with properties different from those of the original substances.**

- In a **chemical change**, matter changes into a new kind of matter. The new matter has different properties from the original matter.
- Burning is one example of a chemical change. When wood burns, elements in the wood combine with oxygen in the air to form new matter. The new matter is ash and gases.
- Tarnishing is another kind of chemical change. Metal tarnishes when it combines with sulfur and forms a dark coating on the metal.

Answer the following question. Use your textbook and the ideas above.

3. Circle the letter of each sentence that is true about chemical changes.

a. Matter changes into a new kind of matter.

b. The new matter has the same properties as the original matter.

c. Burning is one example of a chemical change.

Energy and Matter (pages 73–77)

Forms of Energy (pages 74–76)

Key Concept: **Forms of energy related to changes in matter may include chemical, electromagnetic, electrical, and thermal energy.**

- **Thermal energy** is a kind of energy that is often given off or taken in when matter changes. You feel thermal energy as heat. Thermal energy always flows from warmer objects to cooler objects.
- **Temperature** tells the amount of thermal energy an object has. An object with a lot of thermal energy has a high temperature. An object with little thermal energy has a low temperature.
- **Chemical energy** is a kind of potential energy. Chemical energy is stored in chemical bonds between atoms. When the chemical bonds break and new bonds form, the potential energy changes into another form of energy, such as thermal energy.
- **Electromagnetic energy** is energy that travels in waves through the air. Light and radio waves are electromagnetic energy. **Electrical energy** is the energy of moving charged particles. Electrical energy causes a light bulb to light.

Answer the following questions. Use your textbook and the ideas above.

1. Is the following sentence true or false? Thermal energy flows from warmer objects to cooler objects.

   ____

2. Draw a line from each term to its meaning.

Term	**Meaning**
chemical energy	**a.** energy that travels in waves through the air
electromagnetic energy	**b.** energy stored in chemical bonds between atoms
electrical energy	**c.** energy of moving charged particles

Transforming Energy (page 77)

***Key Concept:* During a chemical change, chemical energy may be changed to other forms of energy. Other forms of energy may also be changed to chemical energy.**

- Chemical energy is stored in the chemical bonds of the elements that make up wood. When wood burns, this chemical energy changes to light and heat.
- Plants change energy from the sun into chemical energy. Plants store the chemical energy as sugar.

Answer the following questions. Use your textbook and the ideas above.

3. Circle the letter of each sentence that is true about the energy changes in burning wood.

a. Light changes to heat.

b. Thermal energy changes to chemical energy.

c. Chemical energy changes to light and heat.

4. Plants change the energy from the sun into

a. electrical energy.

b. chemical energy.

c. electromagnetic energy.

States of Matter (pages 90–95)

Solids (pages 91–92)

Key Concept: **The particles in a solid are closely locked in position and can only vibrate.**

- A **solid** is a kind of matter that has a fixed shape and a fixed volume. Your pencil is a solid. The shape and volume of your pencil will not change if you move the pencil from place to place.
- The different elements and compounds that make up matter are made of particles. The particles of a solid are packed closely together.
- The particles of a solid cannot move from their spot within the solid. However, the particles can move slightly back and forth in place.

Answer the following questions. Use your textbook and the ideas above.

1. Is the following sentence true or false? The particles that make up a solid do not move at all. __________

2. The picture shows two containers with particles of a kind of matter in each. Circle the letter of the container that shows how the particles of a solid are arranged.

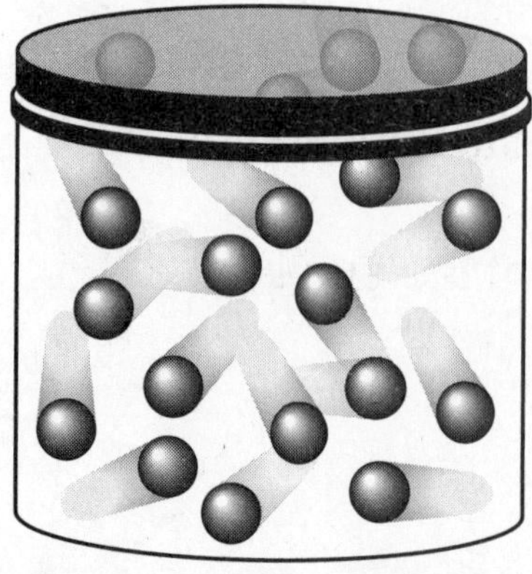

a.

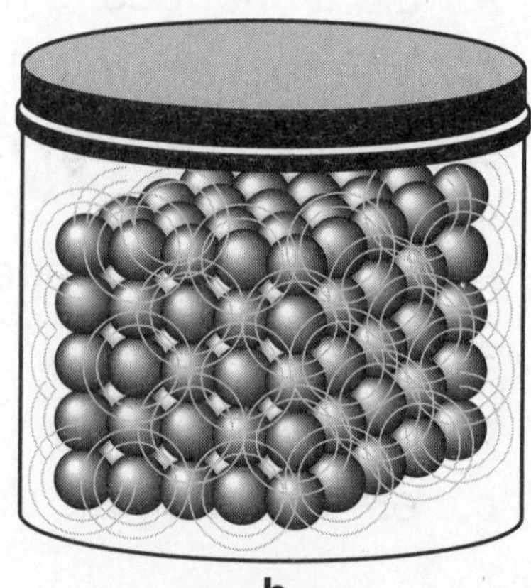

b.

Liquids (pages 93–94)

Key Concept: **Compared to particles in a solid, the particles in a liquid are more loosely connected and can collide with and move past one another.**

- A **liquid** is a kind of matter that has a fixed volume. However, the shape of a liquid changes with the shape of its container.
- Water is a liquid. As you pour water from one cup to another, the shape of the water changes to match the shape of the cup. The volume of the water stays the same.
- The particles of a liquid are packed closely together. However, these particles can move freely.

Answer the following questions. Use your textbook and the ideas above.

3. Which is a liquid?

a. your desk

b. a pencil

c. milk

4. Read each word in the box. In each sentence below, fill in one of the words.

volume	shape	particles

a. A liquid changes ______________________ depending on the liquid's container.

b. A liquid has a definite ______________________ no matter what container the liquid is in.

Gases (page 95)

***Key Concept:* In gases, the atoms and molecules are free to move independently, colliding frequently.**

- As **gas** particles move, they spread apart, filling all the space available.
- A gas is a kind of matter that easily changes volume and shape.
- Air is a gas. When you blow air into a balloon, the air takes the shape of the balloon. When you let the air out of the balloon, the particles spread out into the room.
- Gas particles can move around freely. Gas particles can either spread apart or be squeezed together.

Answer the following questions. Use your textbook and the ideas above.

5. Which is a gas?

  a. fruit juice

  b. air

  c. books

6. Is the following sentence true or false? Gas particles can move around freely. __________

Changes of State (pages 96–101)

Changes Between Solid and Liquid (pages 97–98)

Key Concept: **When a substance melts, the particles in the solid vibrate so fast that they break free from their fixed positions. When a substance freezes, the particles in the liquid move so slowly that they begin to take on fixed positions.**

- When a solid changes to a liquid, the solid is **melting**. Solid ice melts in warm temperatures and forms liquid water.
- When a solid gains thermal energy, the particles of the solid move in place faster. When enough energy is added, the particles break away from their places.
- When a liquid changes to a solid, the liquid is **freezing**. Freezing is just the reverse of melting. Liquid water freezes in very cold temperatures and forms ice.
- When a liquid loses thermal energy, the particles of the liquid slow down. Over time, the particles move into fixed positions. Then, the liquid becomes solid.

Answer the following questions. Use your textbook and the ideas above.

1. Read each word in the box. In each sentence below, fill in the correct word or words.

melting	freezing	thermal energy

   a. When a liquid changes to a solid, the liquid is ______________________.

   b. When a solid changes to a liquid, the solid is ______________________.

2. Fill in the words in the table below to show the relationship between energy and the movement of particles.

Changes Between Solid and Liquid		
Change of State	**Thermal Energy**	**Particles Move**
Melting	added or gained	**b.** __________
Freezing	**a.** __________	slower

3. Is the following sentence true or false? When a liquid becomes a solid, it gains thermal energy. __________

Changes Between Liquid and Gas (pages 98–100)

Key Concept: **Vaporization takes place when the particles in a liquid gain enough energy to move independently, forming a gas. During condensation, the particles in a gas lose enough thermal energy to form a liquid.**

- The change from a liquid to a gas is called **vaporization** (vay puhr ih ZAY shun). At high temperatures, water changes to water vapor. When a puddle of water disappears on a hot, sunny day, the water has changed to water vapor.
- When a liquid gains thermal energy, the particles of the liquid move faster. When enough energy is added, the particles spread far apart. Then, the liquid becomes a gas.

- The change from a gas to a liquid is called **condensation** (kahn dehn SAY shun). When water vapor cools, it becomes liquid water. Dew on the grass in the morning is water vapor in the air that has cooled and become a liquid.
- When gas particles lose thermal energy, they slow down. As the particles slow down, the particles move closer together and form a liquid.

Answer the following questions. Use your textbook and the ideas on page 50 and above.

4. Look at the pictures below. One shows a puddle of water on a sunny day. The other shows drops of dew as they form on grass. Circle the letter of the picture in which vaporization is occurring.

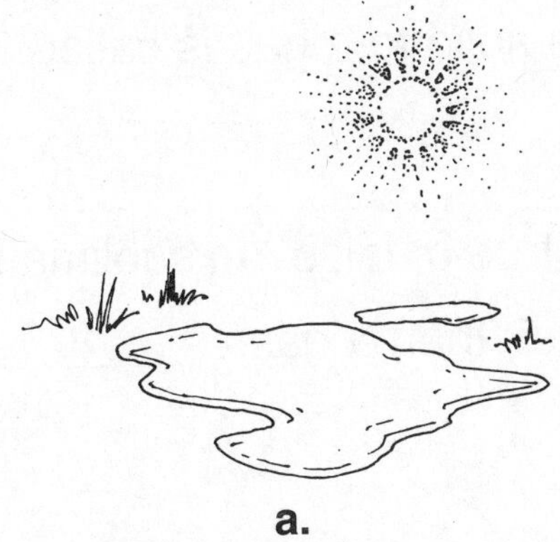

a.

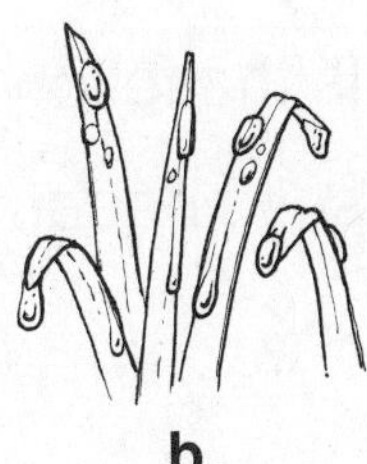

b.

5. Read each word in the box. In each sentence below, fill in one of the words.

make	gain	lose

a. Vaporization takes place when liquid particles ______________________ thermal energy.

b. Condensation takes place when gas particles ______________________ thermal energy.

Changes Between Solid and Gas (page 101)

Key Concept: **During sublimation, particles of a solid do not pass through the liquid state as they form a gas.**

- The direct change from a solid to a gas is called **sublimation** (suhb luh MAY shun). In sublimation, the solid never changes to a liquid. When snow seems to disappear without melting, sublimation has taken place.
- Sublimation takes place when particles on the surface of a solid gain enough thermal energy to break away. The particles have enough energy to spread far apart and form a gas.

Answer the following questions. Use your textbook and the ideas above.

6. The direct change from a solid to a gas is called

______________________.

7. Is the following sentence true or false? In sublimation, a solid becomes a liquid first, then a gas. __________

The Behavior of Gases (pages 103–111)

Measuring Gases (pages 104–105)

***Key Concept:* When working with a gas, it is helpful to know its volume, temperature, and pressure.**

- Volume is the amount of space that matter takes up. The volume of a gas is the same as the volume of its container.
- Temperature tells the amount of thermal energy an object has. Temperature is a measure of the motion of the particles of matter. The faster the particles move, the higher the temperature. Gas particles move very fast.
- As gas particles move, they bump into the sides of their container. The **pressure** of a gas is the strength of its push on the walls of the container. Gas pressure is high when gas particles bump the sides of the container often and hard.

Answer the following questions. Use your textbook and the ideas above.

1. Draw a line from each term to its meaning.

Term	Meaning
pressure	**a.** the amount of space that matter takes up
temperature	**b.** a measure of the motion of particles of matter
volume	**c.** the strength of gas particles bumping into the sides of the container

2. Circle the letter of each sentence that is true about gas behavior.
   a. The volume of a gas is the same as the volume of its container.
   b. The faster that gas particles move, the lower the temperature.
   c. Gas pressure is high when gas particles bump the sides of the container often and hard.

Temperature and Volume (pages 106–107)

Key Concept: **When the temperature of a gas is increased at constant pressure, its volume increases. When the temperature of a gas is decreased at constant pressure, its volume decreases.**

- Charles's law tells how the temperature and the volume of a gas are related when gas pressure stays the same.
- At high temperatures, gas particles move fast and spread far apart. When gas particles move far apart, the gas takes up more space. The volume of the gas is large.
- At low temperatures, gas particles move slowly and close together. When gas particles move close together, the gas takes up less space. The volume of the gas is small.

Answer the following question. Use your textbook and the ideas on page 54.

3. Look at the two balloons. Both balloons are filled with the same amount of gas.

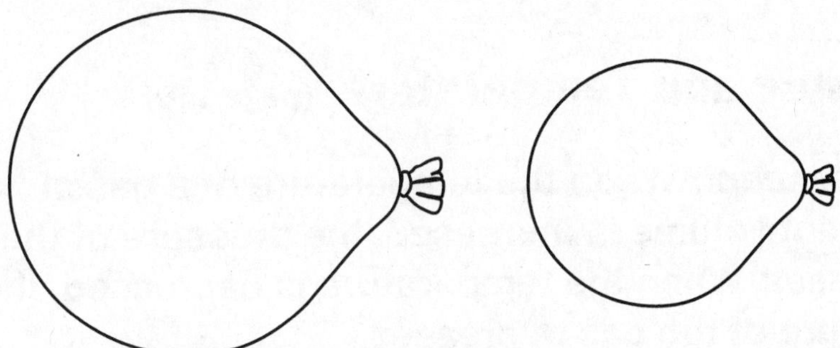

a. Circle the balloon with the larger volume of gas.

b. Underline the balloon at the higher temperature.

Pressure and Volume (pages 108–109)

Key Concept: **When the pressure of a gas at constant temperature is increased, the volume of the gas decreases. When the pressure is decreased, the volume increases.**

- Boyle's law tells how the volume and the pressure of a gas are related when temperature stays the same.
- A gas with decreasing volume has increasing pressure.
- A gas with increasing volume has decreasing pressure.

Answer the following questions. Use your textbook and the ideas above.

4. According to Boyle's law, a gas with decreasing volume has

a. increasing pressure.

b. decreasing pressure.

c. no pressure at all.

5. According to Boyle's law, a gas with increasing volume has
   - **a.** increasing pressure.
   - **b.** decreasing pressure.
   - **c.** no pressure at all.

Pressure and Temperature (page 110)

Key Concept: **When the temperature of a gas at constant volume is increased, the pressure of the gas increases. When the temperature is decreased, the pressure of the gas decreases.**

- At high temperatures, gas particles are moving fast. Fast-moving gas particles hit the walls of the container hard and often. The pressure of the gas is high.
- At low temperatures, gas particles are moving slowly. Slow-moving gas particles hit the walls of the container softly and less often. The pressure of the gas is low.

Answer the following question. Use your textbook and the ideas above.

6. Read each word in the box. In each sentence below, fill in one of the words.

high	fast	low

   - **a.** At high temperature, gas particles have ______________ pressure.
   - **b.** At low temperature, gas particles have ______________ pressure.

Introduction to Atoms

(pages 124–130)

Development of Atomic Theory

(pages 125–127)

Key Concept: **Atomic theory grew as a series of models that developed from experimental evidence. As more evidence was collected, the theory and models were revised.**

- Different scientists suggested different models of the atom from the 1800s until today. Over time, models of the atom changed as scientists made new discoveries.
- An **atom** is the smallest piece of an element.
- An atom contains electrons. An **electron** is a particle with a negative charge. Electrons have almost no mass.
- The **nucleus** (NOO klee us) is the center of an atom. The nucleus contains particles called protons. A **proton** is a particle with a positive charge.
- Electrons can be anywhere in a cloudlike region around the nucleus. Electrons with different energy levels are found in different places around the nucleus. An electron's movement is related to its **energy level,** or the specific amount of energy it has.

Answer the following questions. Use your textbook and the ideas above.

1. The smallest piece of an element is a(an) ______________________.

Elements and the Periodic Table

2. Draw a line from each term to its meaning.

Term	**Meaning**
electron	**a.** a particle of an atom with a positive charge
energy level	**b.** the specific amount of energy an electron has
proton	**c.** a particle of an atom with a negative charge

3. Is the following sentence true or false? Models of the atom changed over time as scientists made new discoveries. __________

4. The picture shows a model of an atom. Circle the nucleus of the atom.

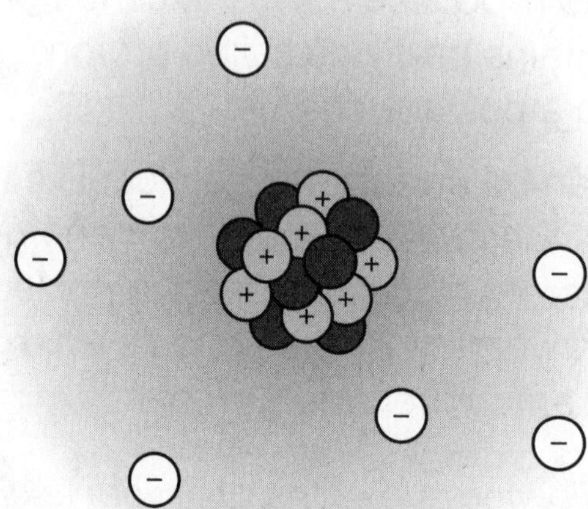

The Modern Atomic Model (pages 128–130)

Key Concept: **At the center of the atom is a tiny, massive nucleus containing protons and neutrons. Surrounding the nucleus is a cloudlike region of moving electrons.**

- A **neutron** is a particle contained in the nucleus. A neutron is electrically neutral, which means that it has no charge.
- In an atom, the number of protons equals the number of electrons. As a result, the positive charge from the protons equals the negative charge from the electrons. The charges balance, making the atom neutral.
- A proton has almost 2,000 times the mass of an electron. A proton and a neutron are about equal in mass.
- Most of an atom's volume is the space in which the electrons move. Atoms themselves are extremely small. The tiniest speck of dust may contain 10 million billion atoms.
- Every atom of an element has the same number of protons. For example, the nucleus of every carbon atom has 6 protons. The **atomic number** of an element is the number of protons in the nucleus of its atoms. The atomic number of carbon is 6.
- The atoms of an element can have a different number of neutrons in the nucleus. An atom with the same number of protons and a different number of neutrons than other atoms of the same element is called an **isotope** (EYE suh tohp). An isotope is identified by its mass number. The **mass number** of an atom is the sum of the protons and neutrons in its nucleus.

Answer the following questions. Use your textbook and the ideas on page 59.

5. Fill in the table below about the particles that make up an atom.

Particles of an Atom		
Particles	**Electric Charge**	**Location in an Atom**
Proton	positive	**a.** __________
Electron	**b.** __________	cloud around nucleus
c. __________	no charge	nucleus

6. Is the following sentence true or false? Every atom of an element has the same number of protons.

____

7. Draw a line from each term to its meaning.

Term	**Meaning**
atomic number	**a.** an atom with the same number of protons and a different number of neutrons than other atoms of the same element
isotope	**b.** the sum of the protons and neutrons in an atom's nucleus
mass number	**c.** the number of protons in the nucleus of an atom of an element

Organizing the Elements (pages 131–137)

Mendeleev's Periodic Table (pages 132–133)

Key Concept: **Mendeleev noticed that a pattern of properties appeared when he arranged the elements in order of increasing atomic mass.**

- Mendeleev knew that some elements had similar physical and chemical properties. When Mendeleev arranged the elements in order of their atomic mass, the properties of the element fell into a pattern.
- The **atomic mass** of an element is the average mass of all the isotopes of that element. The mass number of an atom is equal to the number of protons and neutrons in the nucleus.
- The **periodic table** is a chart of the elements. The periodic table shows the repeating pattern of the chemical and physical properties of all the elements. In the current periodic table, the elements are arranged in order of atomic number.

Answer the following questions. Use your textbook and the ideas above.

1. Draw a line from each term to its meaning.

Term	**Meaning**
atomic mass	**a.** a chart of the elements
periodic table	**b.** the average mass of all the isotopes of an element

2. Is the following sentence true or false? The elements in the current periodic table are arranged in order of atomic mass. __________

The Modern Periodic Table (pages 133–137)

***Key Concept:* The properties of an element can be predicted from its location on the periodic table.**

- A row of elements in the periodic table is called a **period**. As you look at the elements in a period from the left side of the table to the right side, the properties of the elements change in the same way for every period.
- The elements on the left side of a period are metals that react with other elements very easily. Elements in the middle of the period do not react with other elements as easily. Elements at the right end of the table are nonmetals.
- A column of elements in the periodic table is called a **group**. Groups are also called families. The elements in each group have properties that are similar. For example, the elements in Group 1 are metals that react very quickly with water. The elements in Group 18 rarely react at all.

Answer the following questions. Use your textbook and the ideas above.

3. Read each word in the box. In each sentence below, fill in one of the words.

element	period	group

a. A row of elements in the periodic table is called a(an) ____________________.

b. A column of elements in the periodic table is called a(an) ____________________.

4. Look at the outline of the periodic table below. Tell which is a group and which is a period.

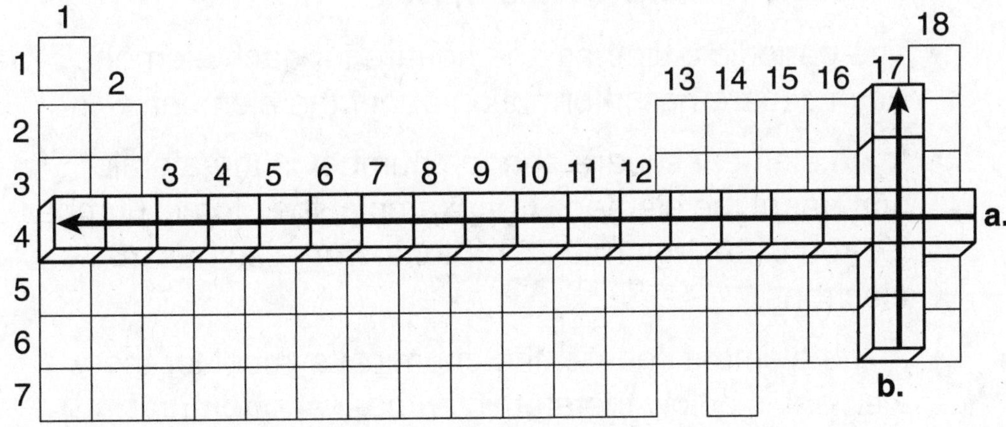

a. ______________________

b. ______________________

5. Circle the letter of each sentence that is true about the periodic table.

a. The elements in a period have properties that are the same.

b. The properties of the elements change in the same way for every period.

c. The elements in each group have properties that are similar.

6. Is the following sentence true or false? Groups are also called families. __________

***Key Concept:* Each square of the periodic table includes the element's atomic number, chemical symbol, name, and atomic mass.**

- The periodic table has one square for each element. Each square has information about the element.
- In an element square, the top number is the atomic number of the element. For example, the atomic number for iron is 26. Iron has 26 protons. Iron also has 26 electrons.
- In the element square, the chemical symbol for the element is below the atomic number. A **chemical symbol** is one or two letters that stand for an element. The chemical symbol for iron is Fe.
- The bottom number in an element square is the atomic mass of the element. The atomic mass of iron is 55.847 amu (atomic mass units).

Answer the following question. Use your textbook and the ideas above.

7. The picture shows an element square from the periodic table. Look at the square to answer the questions.

a. Write the name of the element. __________

b. Write the atomic number of the element.

____

c. Write the chemical symbol of the element.

____

Metals (pages 138–141)

Properties of Metals (pages 138–139)

Key Concept: **The physical properties of metals include luster, malleability, ductility, and conductivity.**

- A **metal** is a shiny element. Gold is a metal.
- Metals are malleable. An object that is **malleable** (MAL ee uh bul) can be hammered or rolled into a flat sheet. Malleability is a physical property.
- Metals are ductile. An object that is **ductile** can be pulled out into a long wire. Ductility is a physical property.
- Most metals are good conductors. **Conductivity** is the ability of an object to move heat or electricity to another object. Conductivity is a physical property.
- **Reactivity** is the ease and speed an atom has combining with other atoms. Reactivity is a chemical property. The atoms of some metals, like sodium, are very reactive. Atoms of gold are not very reactive.

Answer the following questions. Use your textbook and the ideas above.

1. A metal is

a. dull.

b. a poor conductor.

c. shiny.

2. Is the following sentence true or false? Reactivity is a chemical property. __________

3. Draw a line from each term to its meaning.

Term	**Meaning**
malleable	**a.** the ability to move heat or electricity to another object
ductile	**b.** able to be hammered or rolled into a flat sheet
conductivity	**c.** the ease and speed an atom has combining with other atoms
reactivity	**d.** able to be pulled out into a long wire

Metals in the Periodic Table (pages 140–144)

Key Concept: **The reactivity of metals tends to decrease as you move from left to right across the periodic table.**

- The metals in Group 1 of the periodic table are called **alkali metals**. Alkali metals are shiny and soft. These metals are the most reactive group of metals. In nature, these metals are always combined with other elements.
- The metals in Group 2 of the periodic table are called **alkaline earth metals**. Most alkaline earth metals are hard, gray-white, and good conductors. These metals are not as reactive as the metals in Group 1, but are more reactive than the other metals.
- The elements in Groups 3 through 12 are called the **transition metals**. Most transition metals are hard and shiny. All are good conductors. Some transition metals are gold, copper, and iron. These metals are less reactive than the metals in Groups 1 and 2.
- Only some of the elements in Groups 13 through 15 are metals. These metals are not very reactive.

Answer the following questions. Use your textbook and the ideas on page 66.

4. Read each word in the box. In the concept map below, fill in one of the words.

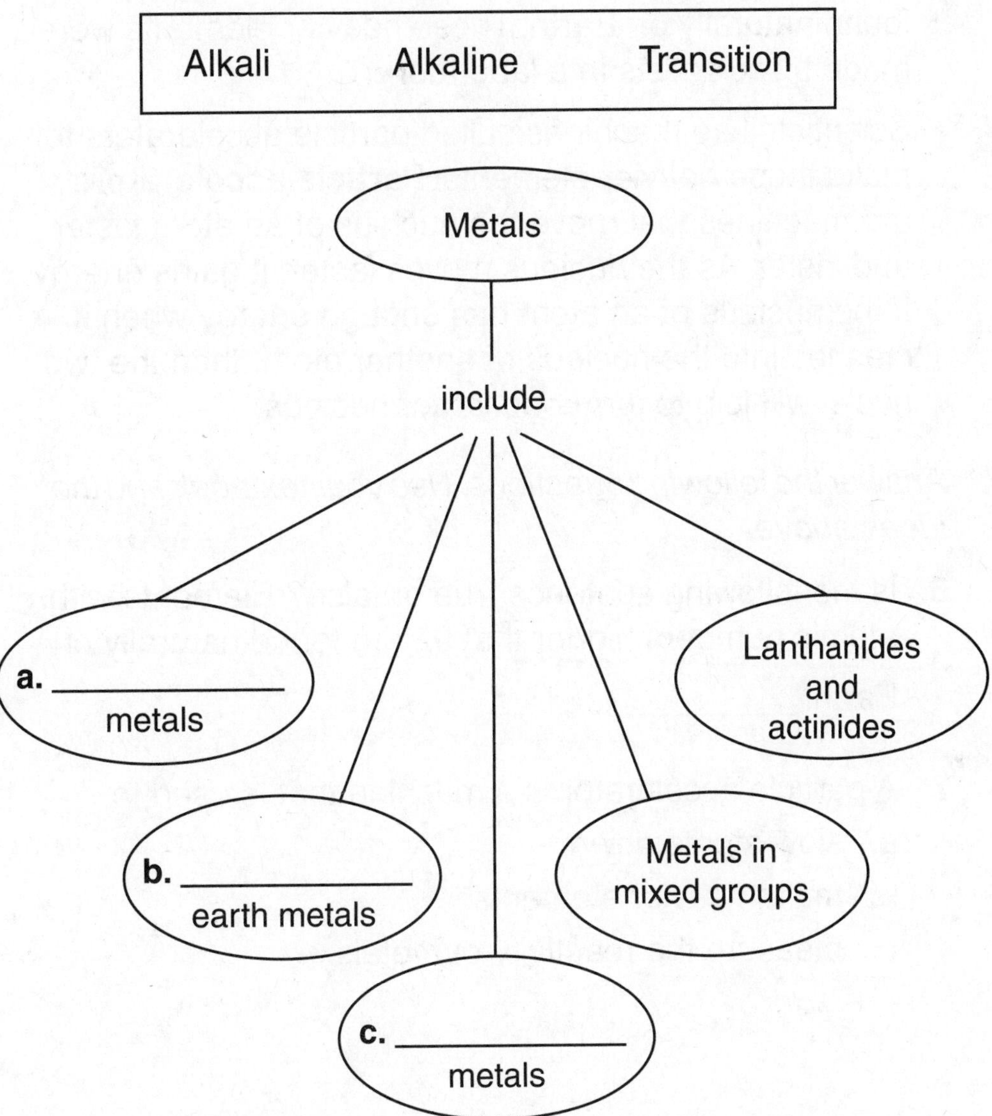

5. Is the following sentence true or false? Metals in Group 1 are the most reactive metals. __________

Synthetic Elements (pages 144–145)

Key Concept: **Scientists make synthetic elements by forcing nuclear particles to crash into one another.**

- Elements with atomic numbers higher than 92 are not found naturally on Earth. These heavier elements were made by scientists in a laboratory.
- Scientists use machines called particle accelerators to make these heavier elements. **Particle accelerators** are machines that move the nucleus of an atom faster and faster. As the nucleus moves faster, it gains energy. If the nucleus of an atom has enough energy when it crashes into the nucleus of another atom, then the two nuclei will join to form one larger nucleus.

Answer the following questions. Use your textbook and the ideas above.

6. Is the following sentence true or false? Elements with atomic numbers higher that 92 are found naturally on Earth. __________

7. A particle accelerator is a machine that is used to

a. slow atoms down.

b. make heavier elements.

c. measure the reactivity of metals.

Nonmetals, Inert Gases, and Semimetals (pages 148–155)

Properties of Nonmetals (pages 149–150)

Key Concept: **Most nonmetals are poor conductors of electric current and heat. Solid nonmetals are dull and brittle.**

- A **nonmetal** is any element that is not a metal. Four nonmetals are gases.
- The physical properties of nonmetals are the opposite of the physical properties of metals. Nonmetals are not shiny. Solid nonmetals break apart easily when hammered. Nonmetals do not move heat or electricity to other objects.
- The chemical properties of nonmetals are also the opposite of the chemical properties of metals. The atoms of nonmetals usually react with the atoms of other elements by gaining electrons or sharing electrons. Most nonmetals react very easily with the atoms of other elements.

Answer the following question. Use your textbook and the ideas above.

1. For each property listed, write *P* if the property describes a physical property of nonmetals. Write *C* if the property describes a chemical property of nonmetals.

   a. very reactive __________

   b. not shiny __________

   c. break apart easily __________

   d. gain or share electrons __________

   e. do not move heat to other objects __________

Families With Nonmetals (pages 150–153)

Groups 14 through 17 in the periodic table contain a mix of nonmetals and other kinds of elements.

- Carbon is the only nonmetal in Group 14. Carbon shares or loses four electrons when it reacts with the atoms of other elements.
- Nitrogen and phosphorus are the two nonmetals in Group 15. Nitrogen and phosphorus gain or share three electrons when reacting with atoms of other elements.
- Oxygen, sulfur, and selenium are the nonmetals in Group 16. These elements gain or share two electrons when reacting with atoms of other elements.
- The elements in Group 17 are called the **halogens**. All the elements in Group 17, except one, are nonmetals. The atoms of halogens gain or share one electron when reacting with the atoms of other elements. All the halogens are very reactive.

Inert Gases (page 154)

Key Concept: **The inert gases tend to be unreactive.**

- The elements in Group 18 are called the **inert gases**. All elements in Group 18 are nonmetals, and all are gases. The atoms of inert gases do not usually gain, share, or lose electrons. Inert gases do not form compounds with other elements.

Hydrogen (page 154)

Hydrogen has the simplest atoms. Hydrogen is too different from other elements to be grouped into a family.

Answer the following questions. Use your textbook and the ideas on page 70.

2. As you move to the right across the periodic table, beginning with Group 16, nonmetals

a. lose more electrons.

b. gain or share fewer electrons.

c. gain or share more electrons.

3. Read each word in the box. In each sentence below, fill in the correct word or words.

metals	halogens	inert gases

a. Elements that are gases and do not usually gain or share any electrons are the

______________________.

b. Elements in Group 17 gain or share one electron and are called the ______________________.

Semimetals (page 155)

***Key Concept:* The most useful property of semimetals is their varying ability to conduct electric current.**

- **Semimetals** are elements that have some properties of metals and some properties of nonmetals. Semimetals are found in the periodic table along the zigzag line between the metals and the nonmetals.
- All semimetals are solids. Semimetals break easily, are hard, and are somewhat reactive.
- Semimetals can move electricity to other objects only at certain temperatures or in certain amounts of light. Because of this property, semimetals are good semiconductors. A **semiconductor** is a material that can move electricity in some conditions but not in other conditions.

Answer the following questions. Use your textbook and the ideas on page 71.

4. Semimetals are elements that have properties of

a. both metals and nonmetals.

b. neither metals nor nonmetals.

c. only gases.

5. Look at the diagram of the periodic table below. Color in the boxes for elements that are semimetals. You may use the periodic table in your book.

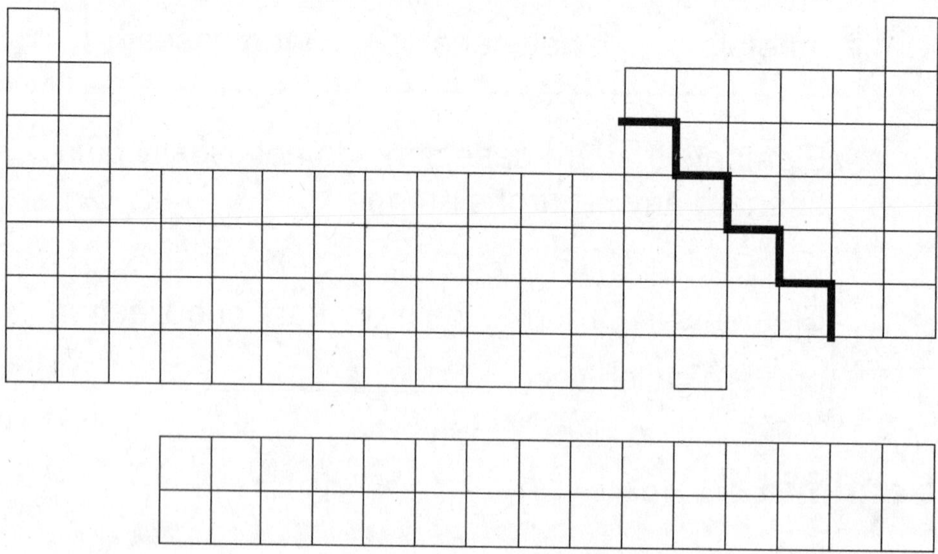

6. A material that can move electricity in some conditions but not in other conditions is called a(an)

a. metal.

b. inert gas.

c. semiconductor.

Radioactive Elements (pages 158–163)

Radioactivity (page 159)

Key Concept: **In 1896, the French scientist Henri Becquerel discovered the effects of radioactive decay by accident while studying a mineral containing uranium.**

- Some isotopes of elements break apart naturally. **Radioactive decay** is a process in which the nuclei of unstable isotopes give off atomic particles and energy.
- Radioactive decay was first discovered by Henri Becquerel. He observed that uranium gives off energy—called radiation—all by itself all the time.
- **Radioactivity** is the giving off of radiation by an unstable nucleus.

Answer the following questions. Use your textbook and the ideas above.

1. Draw a line from each term to its meaning.

Term	Meaning
radioactive decay	**a.** the giving off of radiation by an unstable nucleus
radioactivity	**b.** the process in which nuclei give off atomic particles and energy

2. Is the following sentence true or false? Henri Becquerel discovered radioactive decay by accident. __________

Types of Radioactive Decay (pages 160–161)

Key Concept: **Radioactive decay can produce alpha particles, beta particles, and gamma rays.**

- The three forms of radiation are alpha particles, beta particles, and gamma radiation.
- An **alpha particle** is made up of two protons and two neutrons. When an atom releases an alpha particle, the atom's atomic number decreases by 2. The atom has become a different element.
- A **beta particle** is a fast-moving electron given off by a nucleus. A beta particle forms when an unstable neutron changes into a proton and an electron. The proton stays in the nucleus, and the electron is the beta particle. The atomic number of the atom increases by 1. The atom is a different element.
- **Gamma radiation** is the energy that is released in a nuclear reaction. Whenever an alpha particle or a beta particle is released, gamma radiation is also released. The release of gamma radiation does not change the atomic number of an atom.

Answer the following questions. Use your textbook and the ideas above.

3. Circle the letter of the form of radiation that does NOT change the atomic number of an atom.

a. alpha particle

b. beta particle

c. gamma radiation

4. Is the following sentence true or false? When an atom releases a beta particle, the atom has become a different element. __________

5. The picture shows radioactive decay in which an alpha particle is produced. Circle the alpha particle.

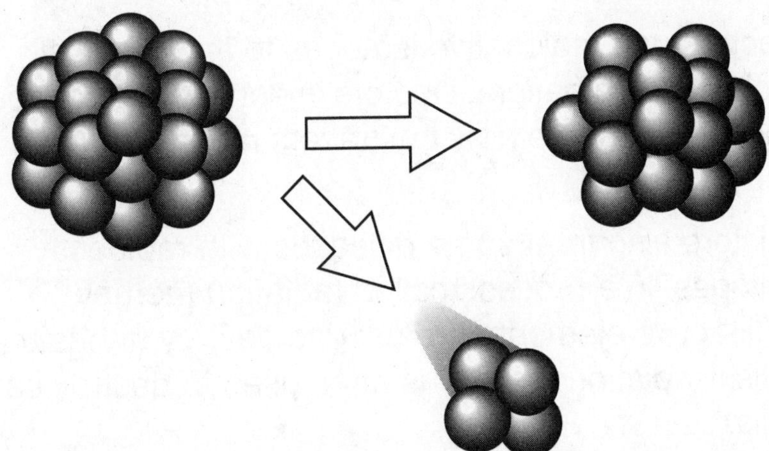

6. After releasing the alpha particle, how has the atom changed? Circle the letter of the correct answer.

a. The atom has not changed.

b. The atomic number of the atom has decreased by 2.

c. The atomic number of the atom has increased by 2.

Using Radioactive Isotopes (pages 161–163)

Key Concept: **Uses of radioactive isotopes include tracing the steps of chemical reactions and industrial processes, and diagnosing and treating disease.**

- Radioactive isotopes have many uses in science and industry.
- Because radiation can be observed, a radioactive isotope can be used to follow the steps of a process. **Tracers** are radioactive isotopes used to trace the steps of a chemical reaction or industrial process.

- In industry, tracers are used to find weak spots in metal pipes. Tracers can be easily observed if they leak out of the pipes.
- Doctors use radioactive isotopes to find medical problems in a patient. Doctors inject traces into a patient and then observe how the tracers move through the body's organs.
- Doctors also treat some diseases with radioactive isotopes. In a process called radiation therapy, radioactive elements are used to destroy unhealthy cells. Radiation therapy is often used to destroy cancer cells.

Answer the following questions. Use your textbook and the ideas on page 75 and above.

7. Radioactive isotopes used to trace the steps of a process are called ________________.

8. Circle the letter of each sentence that is true about using radioactive isotopes.

a. Doctors use radioactive isotopes to find medical problems in a patient.

b. Doctors use radioactive isotopes to find leaks in medical machines.

c. Industry uses radioactive isotopes to find weak spots in metal pipes.

Atoms, Bonding, and the Periodic Table (pages 176–182)

Valence Electrons and Bonding (pages 176–177)

Key Concept: **The number of valence electrons in an atom of an element determines many properties of that element, including the ways in which the atom can bond with other atoms.**

- The **valence** (VAY luns) **electrons** of an atom are the electrons in the highest energy level. These electrons are the farthest away from the pull of the nucleus. So, an atom easily loses valence electrons.
- An **electron dot diagram** shows the number of valence electrons for an element. Each dot in the diagram stands for one valence electron. An element can have from one to eight valence electrons.
- Most atoms are stable when they have eight valence electrons. When atoms are stable, they do not react with other atoms.
- When some atoms react, they gain electrons from another atom to increase their number of valence electrons to eight. Other atoms give up their valence electrons.
- When atoms lose, share, or gain electrons, the atoms react, or join together chemically. A **chemical bond** is the pulling force between two atoms that holds them together.

Answer the following questions. Use your textbook and the ideas above.

1. Is the following sentence true or false? The valence electrons of an atom are the electrons in the lowest energy level closest to the nucleus. __________

2. Look at the electron dot diagrams for sodium (Na), carbon (C), and oxygen (O). Draw a line from each element to its number of valence electrons.

Element	Number of Valence Electrons
Na·	**a.** 6
·C· (4 dots)	**b.** 4
·O: (6 dots)	**c.** 1

3. Circle the letter of each sentence that is true.
   - **a.** Atoms with eight valence electrons easily react with other atoms.
   - **b.** Atoms lose or gain electrons when they react with other atoms.
   - **c.** When atoms form chemical bonds with other atoms, the atoms have joined together chemically.

How the Periodic Table Works (pages 178–182)

Key Concept: **The periodic table reveals the underlying atomic structure of atoms, including the arrangement of the electrons.**

- The periodic table shows the elements arranged in a certain way. The arrangement of elements tells you which elements will combine and how.
- As you look across a period, or row, you can see that the atomic numbers increase from left to right. As the atomic number increases, the number of electrons also increases. This pattern is the same for every period. This pattern means that the elements within a group always have the same number of valence electrons.

- Most of the elements of Group 18—the noble gases—have eight valence electrons. Atoms with eight valence electrons are unlikely to give up electrons to other atoms. As a result, the noble gases do not react easily with other elements.
- Elements of Group 1 react very easily. They can become stable by losing just one valence electron. Elements of Group 17 also react very easily. They can become stable by gaining just one electron.
- How reactive a metal is depends on how easily its atoms lose valence electrons. Among Groups 1 and 2, reactivity increases from top to bottom.
- Elements in the green section of the periodic table are the nonmetals. Most nonmetals are gases at room temperature.
- Semimetals lie along a zigzag line between the metals and nonmetals. These elements can behave as either metals or nonmetals.
- Hydrogen is located in Group 1, but it is considered to be a nonmetal.

Answer the following questions. Use your textbook and the ideas on page 78 and above.

4. Circle the letter of why elements within a group on the periodic table have similar properties.

a. They all have the same number of neutrons in their atoms.

b. They all have the same number of valence electrons in their atoms.

c. They all can behave as metals or nonmetals.

5. Is the following sentence true or false? How reactive a metal is depends on how easily its atoms lose valence electrons. __________

Ionic Bonds (pages 184–189)

Ions and Ionic Bonds (pages 185–186)

Key Concept: **Ionic bonds form as a result of the attraction between positive and negative ions.**

- An atom with an electric charge is called an **ion** (EYE ahn). An atom does not have an electric charge unless it loses or gains an electron.
- If an atom loses an electron, it has more protons. So, the atom becomes an ion with a positive electric charge. If an atom gains an electron, it has more electrons. The atom becomes an ion with a negative electric charge.
- An **ionic bond** is the force of attraction between a positive ion and a negative ion.
- A compound that is made up of positive and negative ions is called an **ionic compound**.

Answer the following questions. Use your textbook and the ideas above.

1. Read each word in the box. In each sentence below, fill in the correct word or words.

ion	ionic bond	valence electron

a. The force of attraction between a positive ion and a negative ion is a(an) ______________.

b. An atom with an electric charge is called a(an) ______________.

2. The picture shows how sodium atoms join with chlorine atoms to form sodium chloride. Circle the ionic compound.

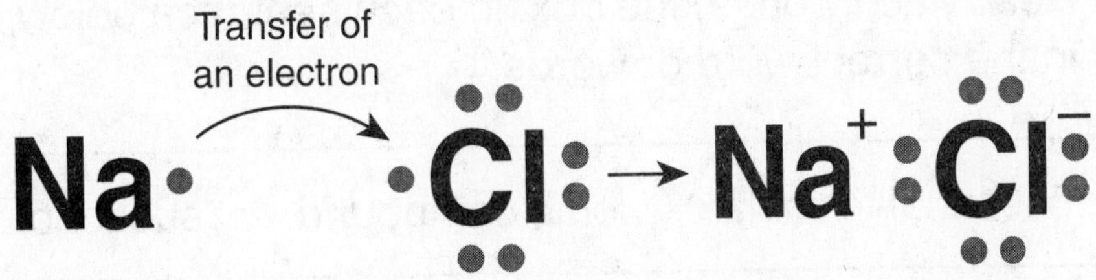

3. In the picture above, which atom lost an electron to become a positive ion? Circle the letter of the answer.

a. Na **b.** Cl **c.** NaCl

Chemical Formulas and Names (page 187)

Key Concept: **When ionic compounds form, the ions come together in a way that balances out the charges on the ions. The chemical formula for the compound reflects this balance. For an ionic compound, the name of the positive ion comes first, followed by the name of the negative ion.**

- A **chemical formula** is a group of symbols that shows how much of each element is in a compound.
- When an ionic compound is named, the positive ion comes first. The negative ion is the second part of the name. For magnesium chloride ($MgCl_2$), magnesium (Mg) is the positive ion and chloride (Cl) is the negative ion.
- When an ionic compound forms, the ions join so that the electric charges equal zero. When magnesium chloride ($MgCl_2$) forms, two chloride ions of 1– are needed to balance the 2+ charge of a magnesium ion.
- A **subscript** tells you the ratio of elements in the compound. For $MgCl_2$, there are two chloride (Cl) ions for every one magnesium (Mg) ion.

Answer the following questions. Use your textbook and the ideas on page 81.

4. Read each word in the box. In each sentence below, fill in the correct word or words.

chemical formula	ionic compound	subscript

a. A number that tells you the ratio of elements in a compound is a(an) ____________________.

b. A group of symbols that shows the elements in a compound is a(an) ____________________.

5. Circle the letter of each sentence that is true about ionic compounds.

a. When an ionic compound forms, the ions join so that the electric charges equal zero.

b. $MgCl_2$ has two ions of Mg.

c. When naming ionic compounds, the negative ion comes first.

Properties of Ionic Compounds (pages 188–189)

Key Concepts: **In general, ionic compounds are hard and brittle with high melting points. When melted or dissolved, they conduct electric current.**

- When ions join together to form ionic compounds, the positive ions are always surrounded by negative ions on all sides. The positive and negative ions form an orderly pattern called a **crystal**.
- Many crystals of ionic compounds are hard and break easily. The crystals have these properties because ionic bonds are very strong.

- Crystals of ionic compounds have high melting points. A lot of heat is needed to give ions enough energy to break away from each other.
- When ionic compounds dissolve in water, the solution can conduct electricity. Crystals of ionic compounds cannot conduct electricity.

Answer the following questions. Use your textbook and the ideas on page 82 and above.

6. Read each word in the box. Use the words to complete the concept map about ionic compounds.

Crystals	Electricity	High	Low

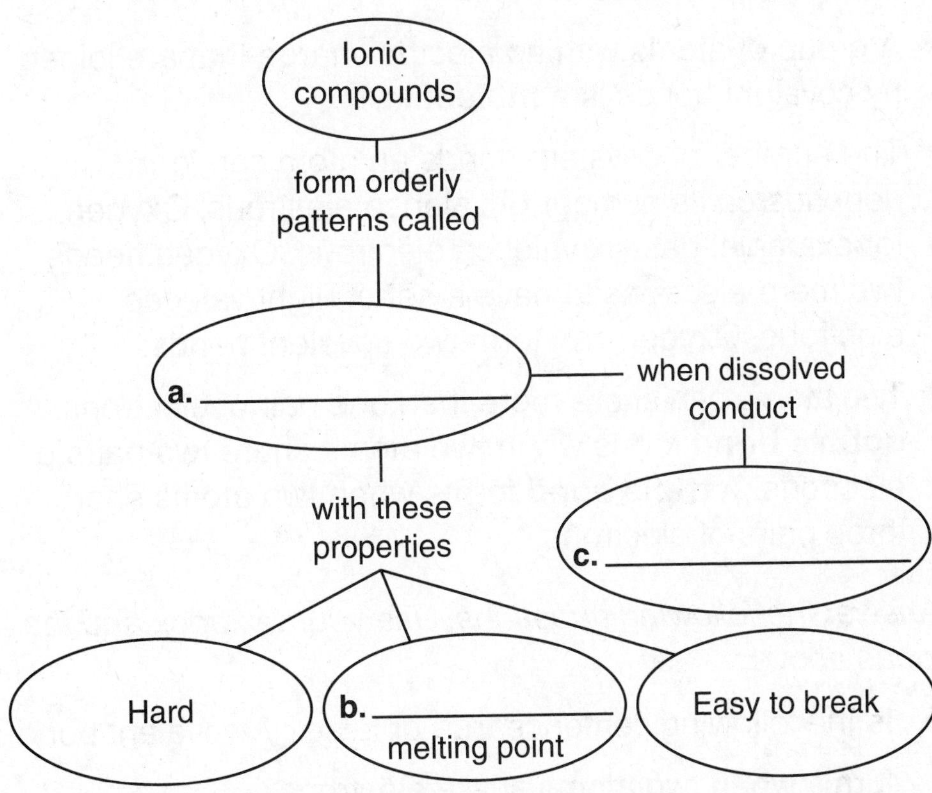

7. Is the following sentence true or false? Ionic bonds are very strong. __________

Covalent Bonds (pages 192–197)

How Covalent Bonds Form (pages 193–194)

Key Concept: **The force that holds atoms together in a covalent bond is the attraction of each atom's nucleus for the shared pair of electrons.**

- Atoms can become more stable by sharing electrons. A **covalent bond** is a chemical bond that forms when two atoms share electrons.
- When an atom shares an electron with another atom, neither atom loses an electron or gains an electron. The positive electric charge of the nucleus of each atom holds the shared electrons in place. Both atoms have a stable set of eight electrons.
- A group of atoms with no electric charge that are joined by covalent bonds is a **molecule**.
- The number of covalent bonds an atom can form depends on its number of valence electrons. Oxygen, for example, has six valence electrons. Oxygen needs two more electrons to have a set of eight valence electrons. Oxygen can form two covalent bonds.
- Two atoms can share more than one pair of electrons. A **double bond** forms when two atoms share two pairs of electrons. A **triple bond** forms when two atoms share three pairs of electrons.

Answer the following questions. Use your textbook and the ideas above.

1. Is the following sentence true or false? A covalent bond forms when two atoms share electrons. __________

2. The picture shows the formation of a covalent bond between two fluorine (F) atoms. Circle the shared electrons.

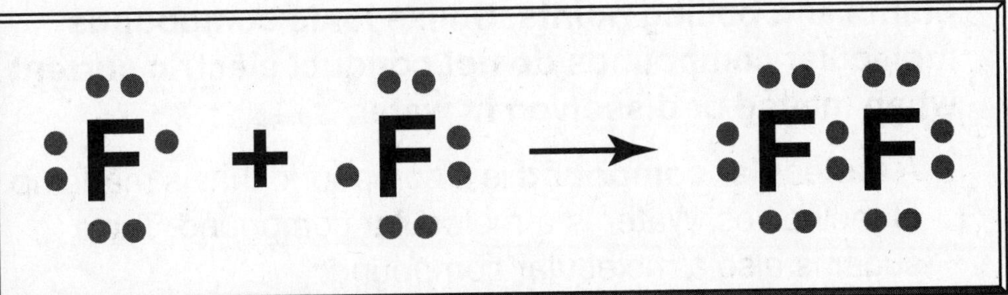

3. Draw a line from each term to its meaning.

Term	Meaning
molecule	**a.** bond that forms when two atoms share two pairs of electrons
double bond	**b.** a group of atoms with no electric charge that are joined by covalent bonds
triple bond	**c.** bond that forms when two atoms share three pairs of electrons

Molecular Compounds (pages 194–195)

***Key Concept:* Compared to ionic compounds, molecular compounds generally have lower melting points and boiling points. Unlike ionic compounds, molecular compounds do not conduct electric current when melted or dissolved in water.**

- A **molecular compound** is a compound that is made up of molecules. Water is a molecular compound. Table sugar is also a molecular compound.
- Covalent bonds hold the atoms of molecules close together. But covalent bonds are not as strong as ionic bonds.
- Compared to ionic compounds, less heat is needed to melt a solid molecular compound.
- Most molecular compounds do not conduct electricity. Molecular compounds do not have any charged particles, so electricity cannot flow.

Answer the following questions. Use your textbook and the ideas above.

4. A compound that is made up of molecules is called a(an) ______________________ compound.

5. Circle the letter of each sentence that is true about molecular compounds.

a. Covalent bonds are stronger than ionic bonds.

b. Compared to ionic compounds, more heat is needed to melt a solid molecular compound.

c. Molecular compounds do not conduct electricity.

Unequal Sharing of Electrons (pages 195–197)

***Key Concept:* Unequal sharing of electrons causes the bonded atoms to have slight electrical charges.**

- Sometimes one atom in a covalent bond pulls more strongly on the shared electrons than the other atom. When this happens, the electrons are no longer equally shared. So, the atom that is pulling the electron pair closer to it has a slightly negative charge. The atom that has a weaker hold on the electron pair has a slightly positive charge.
- A **polar bond** is a covalent bond in which the electrons are not equally shared. The covalent bond between an oxygen atom and a hydrogen atom is a polar bond.
- Not all covalent bonds are polar bonds. If the atoms are the same size, such as two fluorine atoms, then the electrons are pulled equally by the nucleus of each atom. A **nonpolar bond** is a covalent bond in which the electrons are shared equally.

Answer the following questions. Use your textbook and the ideas above.

6. Is the following sentence true or false? The electrons in a covalent bond are always equally shared.

____

7. Circle the letter of a covalent bond in which the electrons are equally shared.

a. polar bond

b. nonpolar bond

c. ionic bond

Bonding in Metals (pages 198–202)

Metals and Alloys (page 199)

Key Concept: **Alloys are generally stronger and less reactive than the pure metals from which they are made.**

- An **alloy** is a mixture of two or more elements, and at least one element is a metal.
- The properties of an alloy are different from the properties of the elements it is made of. For example, pure gold is very soft and easily bent. Gold mixed with copper or silver is much harder. Gold alloys are used for jewelry.
- Alloys are stronger than pure metals. Alloys do not rust as easily as pure metals.

Answer the following questions. Use your textbook and the ideas above.

1. A mixture of a metal with another element is called a(an)

a. polymer.

b. composite.

c. alloy.

2. Is the following sentence true or false? Pure metals are usually stronger than alloys. __________

Metallic Bonding (page 200)

Key Concept: **Metal atoms combine in regular patterns in which the valence electrons are free to move from atom to atom.**

- The physical and chemical properties of metals or metal alloys can be explained by the structure of metal atoms and by the bonding between them.
- Most metals have one, two, or three valence electrons. Metals easily lose electrons. Metal ions have a positive electric charge.
- Solid metals are crystals. Metal atoms in the crystal are very close together. The atoms in a metal crystal are arranged in a specific way.
- In a metal crystal, the atoms exist as positive ions. The valence electrons lost from the ions freely drift around the ions in the crystal. The metal ions are held in place by metallic bonds. A **metallic bond** is the attraction between a positive metal ion and the electrons around it.

Answer the following questions. Use your textbook and the ideas above.

3. Circle the letter of an attraction between a positive metal ion and the electrons around it.

a. ionic bond

b. covalent bond

c. metallic bond

4. Circle the letter of each sentence that is true about metallic bonding.

a. Most metals have one, two, or three valence electrons.

b. Metals easily lose protons.

c. Metal ions have a positive electrical charge.

Metallic Properties (pages 201–203)

***Key Concept:* The "sea of electrons" model of metallic bonding accounts for the malleability, ductility, luster, high electrical conductivity, and high thermal conductivity of solid metals.**

- You can easily change the shape of a metal because the metal ions are not attracted to other metal ions. The ions are attracted only to the loose valence electrons around them. So, the metal ions can be pushed out of position.
- Because metal ions move easily, metals are ductile. Ductile means that a metal can be bent easily and pulled into a wire. Metals are malleable, too. Malleable means that a metal can be rolled into thin sheets or beaten into a shape.
- Electric current is possible when charged particles are free to move. Because the electrons in metals are free to move, metals conduct current easily.
- When light strikes valence electrons, the electrons absorb the light and then give it off again. This makes metals look shiny.
- Heat causes particles to move faster. In metals, the valence electrons are free to move. The electrons in the warmer parts of the metal transfer energy to particles in the cooler parts of the metal.

Answer the following questions. Use your textbook and the ideas above.

5. Is the following sentence true or false? Heat flows easily through metals because the positive metal ions are free to move. __________

Name ______________________ Date ______________ Class __________

6. Look at the pictures of the paper clip and the aluminum pan. Circle the picture that shows that metal is ductile.

7. Read each word in the box. Use the words to complete the concept map about metals.

Ductile	Heat	Luster	Malleable

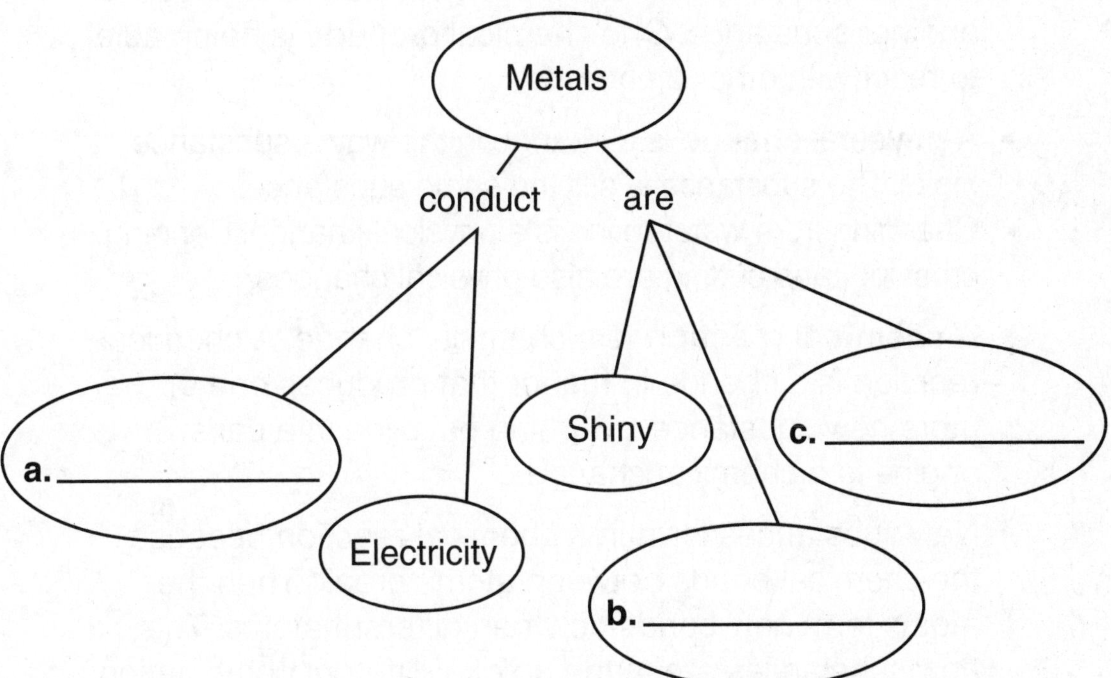

Observing Chemical Change

(pages 214–221)

Matter and Change (pages 215–217)

***Key Concept:* Changes in matter can be described in terms of physical changes and chemical changes. Chemical changes occur when bonds break and new bonds form.**

- A **physical property** is anything that you can see, smell, feel, taste, or hear about a substance.
- Some physical properties are color, hardness, and shine. Melting temperature and being able to conduct electricity are also physical properties.
- A **chemical property** tells how a substance changes to another substance. One chemical property is being able to react with other elements.
- A **physical change** is a change in the way a substance looks. The substance is still the same substance. Changing from water to ice is a physical change. Bending, crushing, and cutting are also physical changes.
- A **chemical reaction** is a chemical change. A chemical reaction is a change in matter that produces one or more new substances. Burning gasoline in a car's engine is a chemical change.
- New substances form in a chemical reaction because the chemical bonds between atoms break. Then the atoms form new bonds between different atoms. The new substances are made up of a different combination of atoms and have different properties.

Answer the following questions. Use your textbook and the ideas on page 92.

1. Circle the letter of a characteristic that describes how a substance can change to another substance.
   a. physical property
   b. chemical property
   c. physical change

2. Look at the pictures of the burning candle and the melting ice cube. Label the physical change and the chemical change.

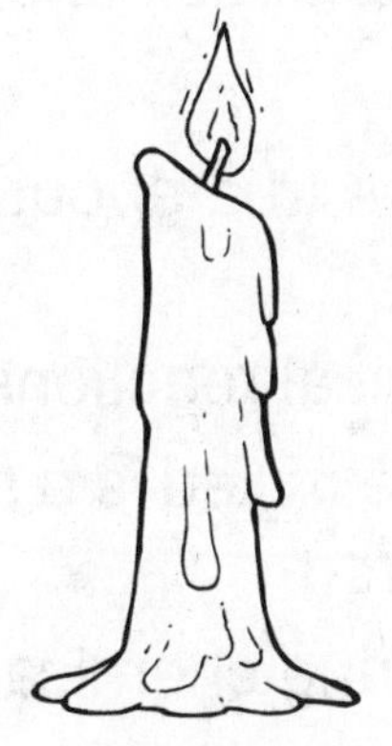

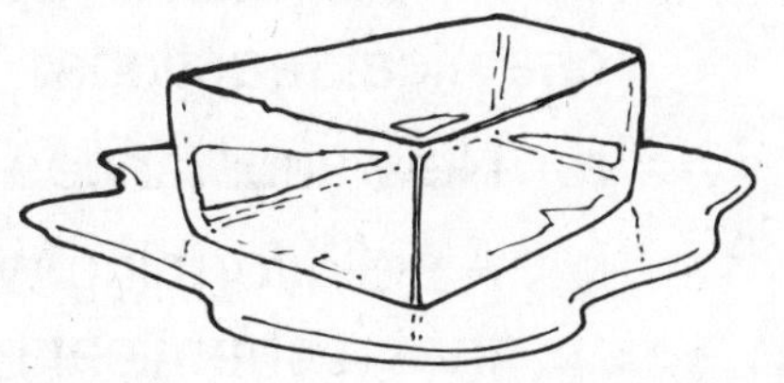

a. ______________________ b. ______________________

3. Is the following sentence true or false? When a chemical reaction occurs, the bonds of a substance break and new bonds form. __________

Evidence for Chemical Reactions (pages 218–221)

Key Concept: **Chemical reactions involve changes in properties and changes in energy that you can observe.**

- You can tell that a chemical reaction has occurred when you observe that a new substance has formed.

- A new substance has formed when the properties have changed. For example, a solid forms when two liquids are mixed.
- Changes in energy are also signs of a chemical reaction. In an **endothermic** (en doh THUR mik) **reaction**, energy is absorbed. Frying an egg is an endothermic reaction. You must keep adding heat, or the reaction will stop.
- An **exothermic** (ek soh THUR mik) **reaction** is a reaction that gives off energy in the form of heat. Burning wood is an exothermic reaction because heat is given off.

Answer the following questions. Use your textbook and the ideas on page 93 and above.

4. Circle the letter of each sentence that is true about chemical reactions.

  a. New substances form during chemical reactions.

  b. A solid forming when two liquids are mixed is a sign that a chemical reaction has occurred.

  c. Changes in energy never occur during chemical reactions.

5. Fill in the table about changes in energy in chemical reactions.

Energy Changes in Chemical Reactions		
Type of Reaction	**Energy Change**	**Example**
Endothermic	energy is **a.** __________	frying an egg
b. __________	energy is given off	burning wood

Describing Chemical Reactions (pages 224–231)

What Are Chemical Equations? (page 225)

Key Concept: **Chemical equations use chemical formulas and other symbols instead of words to summarize a reaction.**

- A **chemical equation** uses symbols to show a chemical reaction in a short, easy way.
- All chemical equations use chemical formulas for the substances in a reaction. For example, the chemical formula for water is H_2O.
- Chemical equations show the substances you begin with and the substances that form at the end. **Reactants** are the substances you begin with. **Products** are the new substances formed in the reaction.
- The general form for a chemical equation is:

  $$\text{Reactant} + \text{Reactant} \rightarrow \text{Product} + \text{Product}$$

  Read the arrow as "yields," which means "forms" or "gives."
- The number of reactants and products can be different. Reactions might have only one reactant or one product. Other reactions might have two or more reactants or products.

Answer the following questions. Use your textbook and the ideas above.

1. Look at the chemical equation below. Circle the reactant.

$$CaCO_3 \rightarrow CaO + CO_2$$

2. Circle the letter of how many products are formed in the reaction in question 1.

a. 1

b. 2

c. 3

Conservation of Matter (pages 226–227)

Key Concept: **In chemical reactions, the number of atoms stays the same no matter how they are arranged. So, their total mass stays the same.**

- The principle of **conservation of matter** states that during a chemical reaction, matter is not created or destroyed. All the atoms present at the start of the reaction are also present at the end of the reaction. So, the products and the reactants have the same number of atoms.
- Some reactions, like burning wood, do not seem to follow the principle of conservation of mass. However, when wood burns, some of the products escape into the air.

Answer the following questions. Use your textbook and the ideas above.

3. What principle states that during a chemical reaction, matter is not created or destroyed?

____

4. Is the following sentence true or false? Matter is not created or destroyed in a chemical reaction.

____

5. The products of a chemical reaction always have the same number of ______________________ as the reactants.

Balancing Chemical Equations

(pages 228–229)

Key Concept: **To describe a reaction accurately, a chemical equation must show the same number of each type of atom on both sides of the equation.**

- Chemical equations must show the same number of atoms for the products and the reactants. Then the equation is balanced.
- To balance a chemical equation, first write the equation. Then count the atoms of each element on both sides of the equation. If the number of atoms is not equal, then the equation is not balanced.
- Balance the equation by adding a coefficient. A **coefficient** (koh uh FISH unt) is a number placed in front of a chemical formula in an equation. The coefficient tells you how many atoms or molecules of a reactant or a product are in the reaction.
- Finally, check the equation. Count the atoms on both sides of the equation again. If the number of atoms on both sides of the equation is equal, the equation is balanced.

Answer the following questions. Use your textbook and the ideas above.

6. Is the following sentence true or false? In the chemical equation $Mg + O_2 \rightarrow MgO$, both sides of the equation have the same number of oxygen atoms. __________

7. For each chemical equation below, fill in the correct number to balance the equation.

a. __________ $H_2 + O_2 \rightarrow 2H_2O$

b. $2\ NaN_3 \rightarrow 2\ Na +$ __________ N_2

Classifying Chemical Reactions (pages 230–231)

Key Concept: **Three general types of chemical reactions are synthesis, decomposition, and replacement.**

- In a **synthesis** (SIN thuh sis) reaction, two or more elements or compounds combine and make a new, more complex product. The reaction of hydrogen and oxygen to make water is a synthesis reaction.

$$2H_2 + O_2 \rightarrow 2\,H_2O$$

- In a **decomposition** (dee KAHM puh zih shun) reaction, compounds are broken down into simpler products. For example, hydrogen peroxide breaks down to water and oxygen.

$$2\,H_2O_2 \rightarrow 2\,H_2O + O_2$$

- In a **replacement** reaction, one element replaces another element in a compound. For example, copper metal is the product when copper oxide is heated with carbon.

$$2\,Cu_2O + C \rightarrow 4\,Cu + CO_2$$

This is a single replacement reaction because only one element, carbon, replaces another element, Cu, in the reaction.

Answer the following questions. Use your textbook and the ideas above.

8. The three categories of chemical equations are synthesis, decomposition, and

________________________.

9. Draw a line from each term to the chemical reaction that is an example of the term.

Term	**Example**
synthesis	**a.** $2\ Cu_2O + C \rightarrow 4\ Cu + CO_2$
decomposition	**b.** $2H_2 + O_2 \rightarrow 2\ H_2O$
replacement	**c.** $2\ H_2O_2 \rightarrow 2\ H_2O + O_2$

10. Fill in the blanks in the concept map about kinds of chemical reactions.

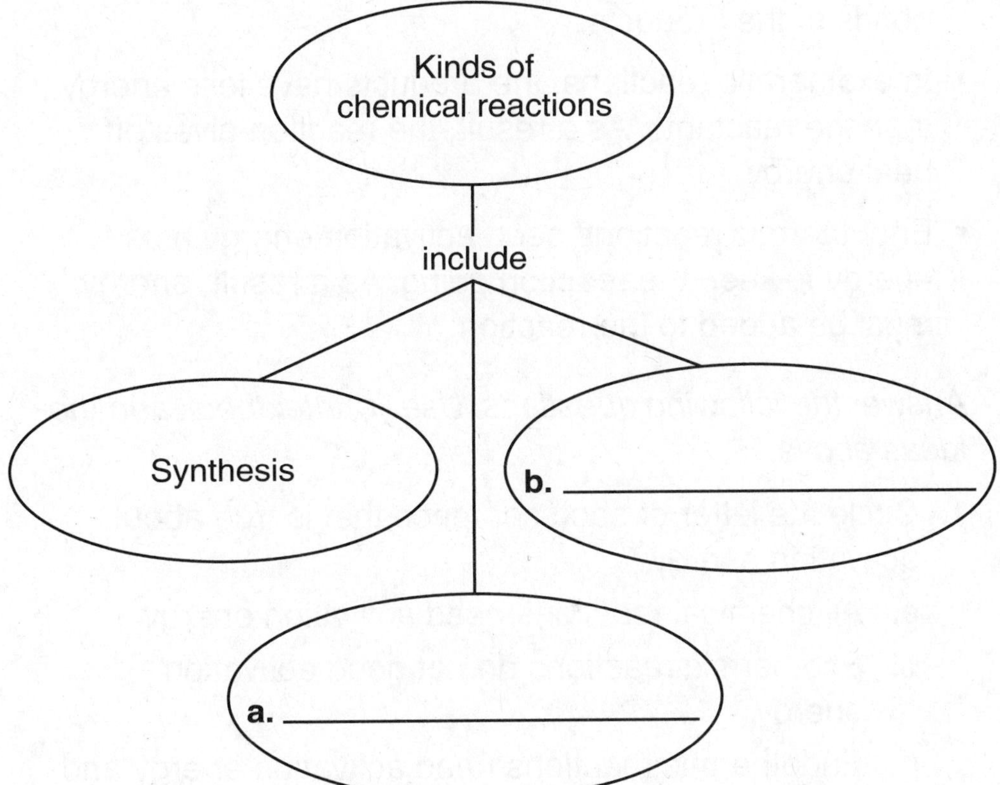

Controlling Chemical Reactions (pages 234–239)

Energy and Reactions (pages 235–236)

Key Concepts: **All chemical reactions require a certain amount of activation energy to get started.**

- **Activation energy** is the smallest amount of energy needed to start a chemical reaction.
- All chemical reactions need a little energy to get started. This energy is used to break the chemical bonds of the reactants. Then, the atoms begin to form the chemical bonds of the products.
- In exothermic reactions, the products have less energy than the reactants. As a result, the reaction gives off heat energy.
- Endothermic reactions need activation energy plus energy to keep the reaction going. As a result, energy must be added to the reaction.

Answer the following questions. Use your textbook and the ideas above.

1. Circle the letter of each sentence that is true about activation energy.

a. All chemical reactions need activation energy.

b. Exothermic reactions do not need activation energy.

c. Endothermic reactions need activation energy and energy to keep going.

Name ______________________ Date ________________ Class ____________

2. Look at the graphs below. Circle the letter of the graph in which the products have less energy than the reactants.

a.

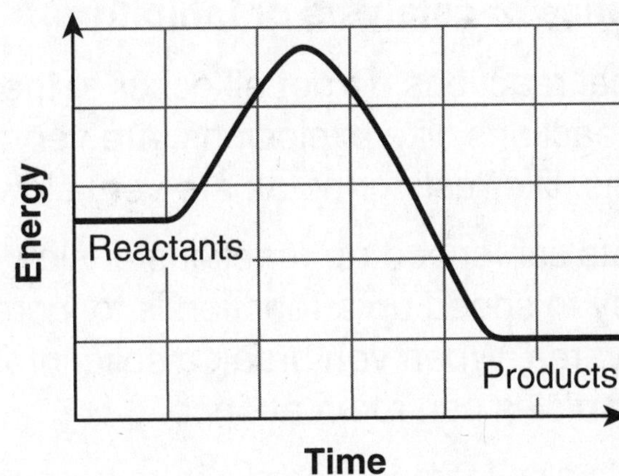

b.

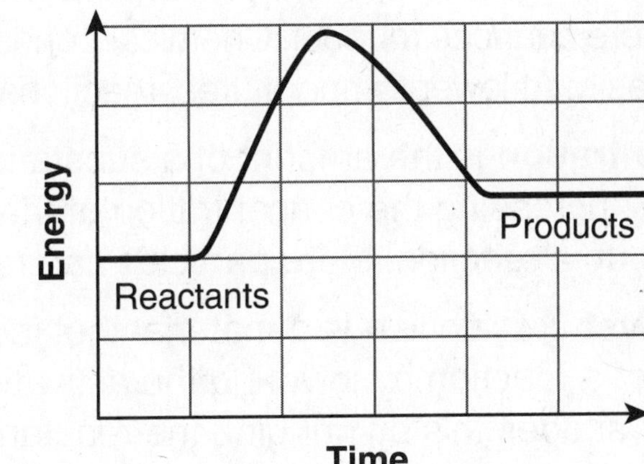

3. Draw a line from each term to its meaning.

Term	**Meaning**
activation energy	**a.** the products have more energy than the reactants
endothermic reaction	**b.** the products have less energy than the reactants
exothermic reaction	**c.** required to start a chemical reaction

Rates of Chemical Reactions (pages 237–239)

Key Concept: **Factors that affect rates of reaction include surface area, temperature, concentration, and the presence of catalysts or inhibitors.**

- Chemical reactions do not all occur at the same rate. Some reactions, like explosions, are very fast. Other reactions, like rusting metal, are very slow.
- Chemists can speed up reactions or slow them down. One way to speed up a reaction is to increase the surface area. When you break a solid into small pieces, more particles can react at once.
- Chemists also increase temperature to speed up a reaction. At higher temperatures, particles move faster and have more chances to react. Chemical bonds also break more easily. At lower temperatures, reactions slow down.
- **Concentration** is the amount of a substance in a given volume. Increasing the concentration of the reactants speeds up a reaction. More particles can react at once.
- A **catalyst** (KAT uh list) is a material that increases the speed of a reaction by lowering the activation energy. A catalyst does this by bringing the reactants close together. A catalyst is not changed in a reaction, so a catalyst is not a reactant.
- An **inhibitor** is a material used to slow down a reaction. Most inhibitors work by keeping reactants away from each other.

Answer the following questions. Use your textbook and the ideas above.

4. Is the following sentence true or false? All chemical reactions occur at the same speed. __________

5. Complete the table. Write *F* if the chemical reaction will go faster. Write *S* if the chemical reaction will slow down.

Controlling Speeds of Chemical Reactions	
Reaction Conditions	**Reaction Occurs Faster or Slower?**
Surface area increases	**a.** ____________
Temperature increases	**b.** ____________
Temperature decreases	**c.** ____________
Concentration increases	**d.** ____________

6. Draw a line from each term to its meaning.

Term	**Meaning**
concentration	**a.** a material that slows down a reaction
catalyst	**b.** a material that speeds up a reaction
inhibitor	**c.** the amount of a substance in a given volume

Fire and Fire Safety (pages 242–245)

Understanding Fire (pages 243–244)

***Key Concept:* Three things necessary to start and maintain a fire are fuel, oxygen, and heat.**

- Fire is caused by combustion. **Combustion** is a very fast reaction between oxygen and a fuel. A **fuel** is a material that gives off energy when it burns. Oil, wood, and gasoline are fuels.
- A fire cannot start unless there is fuel, oxygen, and heat. Oxygen comes from the air. Heat gives the activation energy needed to start combustion. The heat from a lighted match or an electric spark can start a fire.
- A fire will continue to burn as long as it has fuel, oxygen, and heat.
- Firefighters put out fires by removing fuel, oxygen, or heat. Water covers the fuel and keeps it from getting oxygen from the air. The evaporation of water uses a lot of heat, causing the fire to cool. Without heat, there is not enough energy to keep combustion going. The fire goes out.

Answer the following questions. Use your textbook and the ideas above.

1. A material that releases energy when it burns is called a(an) ____________________.

2. A very fast reaction between oxygen and a fuel is called ____________________.

3. Look at the fire triangle. Then circle the letter of what is missing from the fire triangle.
   a. Catalyst
   b. Inhibitor
   c. Heat

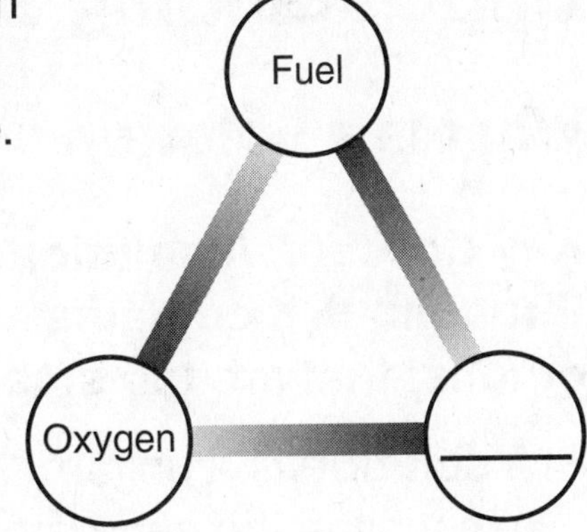

Home Fire Safety (pages 244–245)

Key Concept: **If you know how to prevent fires in your home and what to do if a fire starts, you are better prepared to take action.**

- You can control a small fire by using the fire triangle. You can smother a fire, or keep the fire from getting oxygen.
- A small fire is easy to control. You can cool a match just by blowing on it.
- A fire that is growing as you fight it is out of control. Get away from the fire and call the fire department.
- The best way to stop a fire is to prevent one from starting. Store items that burn easily in places far from sources of flames.

Answer the following question. Use your textbook and the ideas above.

4. Circle the letter of each sentence that is true about fire safety.
   a. You can smother a fire by getting oxygen to it.
   b. If a fire gets out of control, you should call the fire department.
   c. The best way to stop a fire is to prevent one from starting.

Understanding Solutions (pages 256–261)

What Is a Solution? (pages 256–257)

Key Concept: **A solution has the same properties throughout. It contains solute particles (molecules or ions) that are too small to see.**

- A **solution** is a uniform mixture. In a solution, you cannot see the separate parts of the mixture. All samples of a solution have the same properties. Tree sap is a solution. Soft drinks are solutions, too.
- A solution has two parts. The **solvent** is the largest part of a solution. The solvent dissolves the other parts of a solution. Water is the solvent in soft drinks and tree sap.
- The **solute** is the smaller part of a solution. The solute is dissolved by the solvent. Sugar is one of the solutes in soft drinks and tree sap.
- Many solutions are not made of liquids. Air is a mixture of gases. Brass is a mixture of solids.

Answer the following questions. Use your textbook and the ideas above.

1. Draw a line from each term to its meaning.

Term	Meaning
solution	**a.** the largest part of the solution
solvent	**b.** the smaller part of a solution
solute	**c.** a uniform mixture

2. Is the following sentence true or false? Air is an example of a solution. __________

Colloids and Suspensions (page 258)

Key Concept: **A colloid contains larger particles than a solution. A suspension has even larger particles and does not have the same properties throughout.**

- A **colloid** (KAHL oyd) is a mixture that contains small, undissolved particles that do not settle out. Examples of colloids are gelatin, milk, and fog.
- The particles in a colloid are too small to be seen. However, the particles in a colloid are large enough to scatter light. You cannot see clearly through a colloid.
- A **suspension** (suh SPEN shun) is a mixture in which the particles are large enough to see. An example of a suspension is orange juice with pulp.
- Because the particles in a suspension are so large, the particles are easy to remove by filtering or by letting them settle out.

Answer the following questions. Use your textbook and the ideas above.

3. Read each word in the box. In each sentence below, fill in one of the words.

colloid	solution	suspension

a. A mixture in which the particles are large enough to see is a ____________________.

b. A mixture that contains small, undissolved particles that do not settle out is a ____________________.

4. Circle the letter of the kind of mixture that has the largest particles.

a. solution **b.** colloid **c.** suspension

Particles in a Solution (page 259)

***Key Concept:* When a solution forms, particles of the solvent surround and separate the particles of the solute.**

- Table salt is an ionic compound. When an ionic compound mixes with water, water molecules completely surround the positive ions and the negative ions. The positive ions and negative ions are separated from each other.
- Table sugar is a molecular compound. When sugar mixes with water, the covalent bonds within its molecules are not broken. Sugar breaks up into individual neutral sugar molecules. The individual sugar molecules are completely surrounded by water molecules and are separated from each other.
- A solution of ionic compounds in water can conduct electricity. Separate positive ions and negative ions let electricity flow.
- A solution of molecular compounds in water cannot conduct electricity. If no ions are present, as in a sugar solution, current will not flow.

Answer the following questions. Use your textbook and the ideas above.

5. Circle the letter of each sentence that is true about particles in a solution.

a. An ionic compound separates into positive ions and negative ions when it dissolves.

b. A molecular compound separates into neutral molecules when it dissolves.

c. Table sugar is an ionic compound.

6. Is the following sentence true or false? A solution of ionic compounds in water cannot conduct electricity.

____

Effects of Solutes on Solvents

(pages 260–261)

***Key Concept:* Solutes lower the freezing point and raise the boiling point of a solvent.**

- You can change the freezing point of water by adding solutes to the water. You can also change the boiling point of water by adding solutes to the water.
- Solutes lower the freezing point of a solvent. Pure water freezes at 0°C. A solution of salt water freezes at a lower temperature. The salt particles (solute) make it harder for the water molecules to form crystals.
- Solutes raise the boiling point of a solvent. Pure water boils at 100°C. A solution of salt water boils at a higher temperature. The salt particles (solute) make it harder for water molecules to gain energy and escape into the air as a gas. More energy is needed.

Answer the following questions. Use your textbook and the ideas above.

7. Look at the pictures of water particles. Which picture shows liquid water in a saltwater bay?

    ____

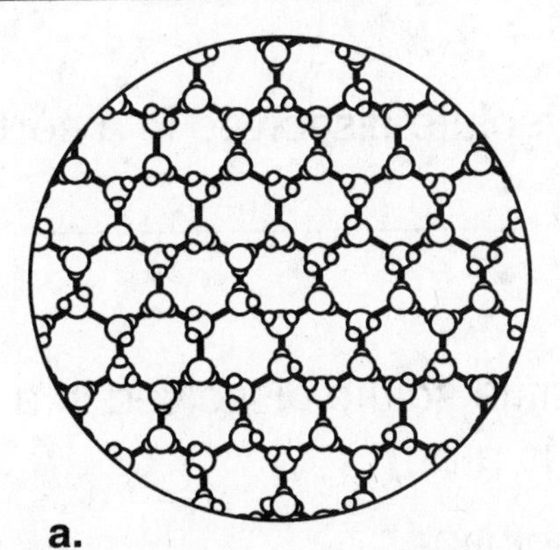

a.

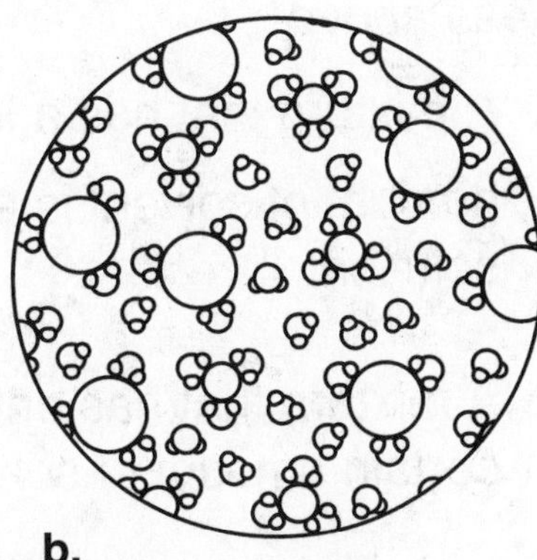

b.

8. Is the following sentence true or false? Water boils at lower temperatures when salt is added to it.

    ____

Concentration and Solubility

(pages 262–267)

Concentration (pages 262–263)

Key Concept: **To measure concentration, you compare the amount of solute to the total amount of solution.**

- A **concentrated solution** is a mixture that has a lot of solute dissolved in a certain amount of solvent. Maple syrup is a concentrated solution.
- A **dilute solution** is a mixture that has only a little solute dissolved in a certain amount of solvent. Tree sap is a dilute solution.
- A solution becomes more concentrated if you add solute or take away solvent. A solution becomes more dilute if you add solvent.
- You can describe concentration in a few ways. You can measure the mass of the solute compared to the mass or volume of the solvent. Or you can measure the volume of the solute compared to the volume of the solvent.

Answer the following questions. Use your textbook and the ideas above.

1. A mixture that has a lot of solute dissolved in a certain amount of solvent is a(an) ______________________ solution.

2. A mixture that has only a little solute dissolved in a certain amount of solvent is a(an) ______________________ solution.

3. Is the following sentence true or false? You can change the concentration of a solution by adding solute. ___________

Solubility (pages 263–264)

Key Concept: **Solubility can be used to help identify a substance because it is a characteristic property of matter.**

- **Solubility** is a measure of how much solute can dissolve in a solvent at a given temperature.
- A **saturated solution** is a solution that has so much solute that no more solute will dissolve. A saturated solution is filled up with solute.
- An **unsaturated solution** is a solution that can still dissolve more solute. An unsaturated solution has room to add more solute.
- Solubility tells you how much solute you can dissolve before a solution becomes saturated, or filled up.
- Solubility is a characteristic property of a substance. You can use solubility to identify an unknown substance.

Answer the following questions. Use your textbook and the ideas above.

4. ____________________ tells how much solute can dissolve in a solvent at a given temperature.

5. A solution that cannot hold any more solute may be described as ____________________.

Factors Affecting Solubility (pages 264–267)

Key Concept: **Factors that affect the solubility of a substance include pressure, the type of solvent, and temperature.**

- Pressure affects the solubility of gases. At high pressure, more gas dissolves. Think of opening a soft drink bottle. When you remove the cap, the pressure inside the bottle gets lower and the gas escapes.
- The kind of solvent affects solubility. For example, oil and water do not mix. Oil is a nonpolar compound. Water is a polar compound. Polar compounds and nonpolar compounds do not mix well.
- Temperature affects solubility. At high temperatures, more solid can dissolve. For example, more sugar dissolves in boiling water than in cold water. When the solution cools, the extra sugar stays dissolved. The solution is a **supersaturated solution** because the solution is holding more solute than it normally could. The solution is "super full."

Answer the following question. Use your textbook and the ideas above.

6. Complete the concept map about solubility.

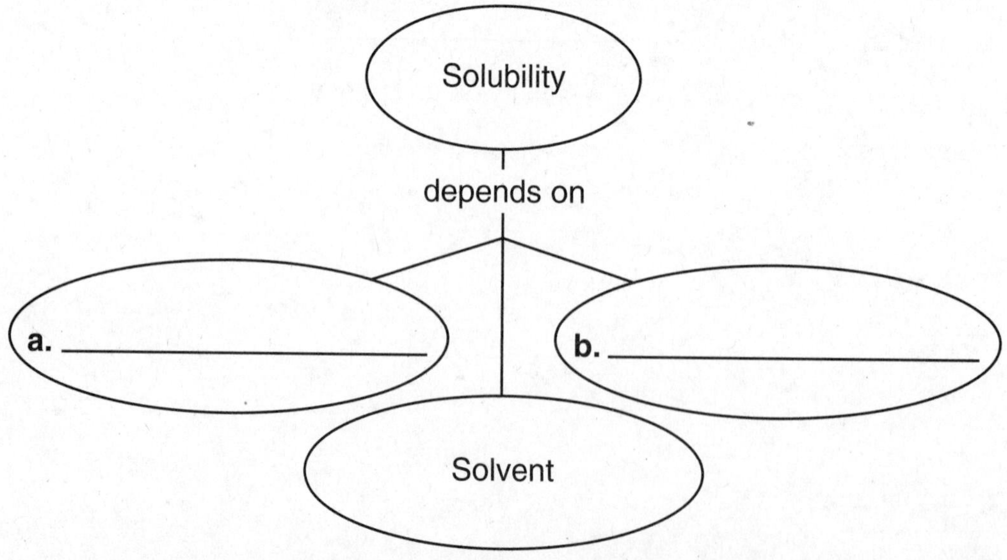

Describing Acids and Bases

(pages 268–273)

Properties of Acids (pages 268–270)

Key Concept: **An acid is a substance that tastes sour, reacts with metals and carbonates, and turns blue litmus paper red.**

- An **acid** is a compound that tastes sour, reacts with metals, and turns blue litmus paper red. Two examples of acids are hydrochloric acid and acetic acid.
- Acids tastes sour. Citrus fruits like lemons and grapefruit are acidic. Never taste a chemical to identify it as an acid.
- Acids are corrosive. **Corrosive** means to wear away other materials. When an acid reacts with some metals, the metals seem to disappear.
- Litmus paper is an indicator. An **indicator** is a compound that changes color when in contact with an acid or a base. Acids turn blue litmus paper red.

Answer the following questions. Use your textbook and the ideas above.

1. Circle the letter of what is NOT a property of an acid.

   a. sour taste

   b. reacts with some metals

   c. turns litmus paper blue

2. A compound that changes color when in contact with an acid or a base is a(an) ______________________.

3. Because acids wear away some metals, acids are ______________________.

Properties of Bases (page 271)

***Key Concept:* A base is a substance that tastes bitter, feels slippery, and turns red litmus paper blue.**

- A **base** is a compound that tastes bitter, feels slippery, and turns litmus paper blue. Two examples of bases are sodium hydroxide and ammonia.
- Bases taste bitter. Soaps and detergent taste bitter. Never taste a substance to identify it as a base.
- Bases feel slippery. Soap feels slippery between your fingers. Strong bases can burn your skin. Never touch a substance to identify it as a base.
- Bases turn red litmus paper blue. An easy way to remember this is to remember the letter *b.*

Answer the following questions. Use your textbook and the ideas above.

4. Circle the letter of what is NOT a property of a base.

a. sour taste

b. slippery feel

c. turns litmus paper blue

5. Is the following sentence true or false? It is safe to taste or touch an unknown substance to identify it as a base. __________

Uses of Acids and Bases (pages 272–273)

***Key Concept:* Acids and bases have many uses around the home and in industry.**

- Acids found in foods like tomatoes and oranges have important jobs in your body.
- Fertilizer and batteries contain acids.

- Baking soda is a base that makes cakes and cookies light and fluffy.
- Many cleaning products have bases. Cement is made with bases.

Answer the following questions. Use your textbook and the ideas on page 114 and above.

6. The picture shows two foods, a lemon and a cake. Circle the food that has an acid. Underline the food that is made with a base.

7. Draw a line from each type of compound to its use. Compounds can be used more than once.

Compound	**Use**
acid	**a.** fertilizer
	b. cleaning products
base	**c.** cement
	d. batteries

Acids and Bases in Solution (pages 274–279)

Acids in Solution (pages 274–275)

Key Concept: **An acid is any substance that produces hydrogen ions (H^+) in water.**

- When acids are mixed with water, **hydrogen ions (H^+)** and negative ions form.
- Hydrogen ions cause the properties of acids.

Answer the following questions. Use your textbook and the ideas above.

1. A(An) ______________________ produces hydrogen ions (H^+) in water.

2. The properties of acids are caused by ______________________.

Bases in Solution (page 275)

Key Concept: **A base is any substance that produces hydroxide ions (OH^-) in water.**

- The **hydroxide ion (OH^-)** is a negative ion made of oxygen and hydrogen.
- When bases dissolve in water, the positive ions and negative ions separate.

Answer the following questions. Use your textbook and the ideas above.

3. A(An) ______________________ produces hydroxide ions (OH^-) in water.

4. The hydroxide ion (OH^-) is made of ______________________ and hydrogen.

Strength of Acids and Bases (pages 276–277)

Key Concept: **A low pH tells you that the concentration of hydrogen ions is high. In contrast, a high pH tells you that the concentration of hydrogen ions is low.**

- Acids may be strong or weak. A strong acid produces more hydrogen ions (H^+) when dissolved in water than an equal concentration of weak acid.
- Bases may be strong or weak. A strong base produces more hydroxide ions (OH^-) when dissolved in water than an equal concentration of weak base.
- The **pH scale** is a range of numbers from 0 to 14. The pH tells the concentration of hydrogen ions in a solution. If a solution has a high concentration of hydrogen ions, it is an acid. A pH lower than 7 is acidic.
- If a solution has a low concentration of hydrogen ions, it is a base. A pH higher than 7 is basic.
- A pH equal to 7 means that the solution is neither an acid nor a base. The solution is neutral. Pure water has a pH of 7.

Answer the following questions. Use your textbook and the ideas above.

5. Circle the letter of what a strong acid has.

a. many hydroxide ions (OH^-)

b. many hydrogen ions (H^+)

c. few hydrogen ions (H^+)

6. Look at the pH scale below. Circle the part of the scale where the basic substances are.

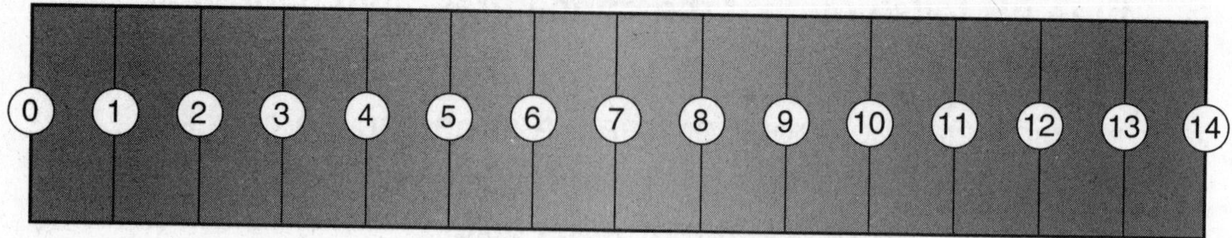

Acid-Base Reactions (pages 278–279)

Key Concept: **In a neutralization reaction, an acid reacts with a base to produce a salt and water.**

- A reaction between an acid and a base is called a **neutralization reaction**. An example of a neutralization reaction is:

$$HCl + NaOH \rightarrow H_2O + Na^+ + Cl^-$$

- The reactants in a neutralization reaction are an acid (HCl) and a base (NaOH).
- One product of a neutralization reaction is water. The other product is a salt. A **salt** is any ionic compound made from the positive ion of a base and the negative ion of an acid.

Answer the following questions. Use your textbook and the ideas above.

7. A reaction between an acid and a base is called a(an) ______________________ reaction.

8. One product of a neutralization reaction is a(an) ______________________.

Properties of Carbon (pages 292–295)

Carbon Atoms and Bonding (page 293)

Key Concept: **Because of its unique ability to combine in many ways with itself and other elements, carbon has a central role in the chemistry of living organisms.**

- The atomic number of carbon is 6. An atom of carbon has six protons and six electrons. Four of the electrons are valence electrons. A carbon atom is stable when it has four more valence electrons.
- Carbon is able to form four chemical bonds with other elements and with itself.
- Carbon atoms can form straight chains, branched chains, and rings.

Answer the following questions. Use your textbook and the ideas above.

1. How many valence electrons does carbon have?

a. 2 **b.** 4 **c.** 6

2. Draw a line from each term to the diagram that shows what term looks like.

Term	Diagram
branched chain	**a.** –C–C–C–
ring	**b.** –C–C(–C)(–C–)–C–C–
straight chain	**c.** six-carbon ring (C–C ring)

Forms of Pure Carbon (pages 294–295)

Key Concept: **Diamond, graphite, fullerenes, and nanotubes are four forms of the element carbon.**

- Pure carbon is found in different forms. These forms of carbon exist because of the ways that carbon can form chemical bonds.
- **Diamond** is the hardest mineral. Carbon atoms form diamond crystals only at very high temperatures and high pressures.
- **Graphite** is a form of carbon in which each carbon atom is tightly bonded to three other carbon atoms in flat layers. These layers easily slide past each other.
- **Fullerene** is a form of carbon that scientists made. The carbon atoms in a fullerene are arranged in the shape of a hollow sphere.
- A **nanotube** is another form of carbon made by scientists. In a nanotube, carbon atoms are arranged in the shape of a long, hollow tube.

Answer the following questions. Use your textbook and the ideas above.

3. Is the following sentence true or false? Pure carbon is found in different forms because of the way it forms bonds. __________

4. Draw a line from each form of carbon to the arrangement of its atoms.

Form of Carbon	Arrangement of Atoms
diamond	**a.** hollow sphere
graphite	**b.** crystal
fullerene	**c.** flat layers
nanotube	**d.** long, hollow tube

Carbon Compounds (pages 296–304)

Organic Compounds (page 297)

Key Concept: **Many organic compounds have similar properties in terms of melting points, boiling points, odor, electrical conductivity, and solubility.**

- **Organic compounds** are compounds that contain carbon. Organic compounds are found in all living things. They are also found in products made by living things, such as wood and cotton. Organic compounds are also found in things made by people, such as gasoline and plastics.
- Organic compounds have low melting points and low boiling points. So, many organic compounds are liquids or gases at room temperature.
- Organic liquids often have strong odors.
- Organic compounds do not conduct electricity.
- Organic compounds do not dissolve well in water.

Answer the following questions. Use your textbook and the ideas above.

1. Circle the letter of the correct answer. An organic compound is a compound that

a. is made only by people.

b. is made only by plants.

c. contains carbon.

2. Circle the letter of each sentence that is true about organic compounds.

a. Organic compounds are always solids at room temperature.

b. Organic compounds conduct electricity.

c. Organic compounds do not dissolve well in water.

Hydrocarbons (pages 298–301)

Key Concept: **Like many other organic compounds, hydrocarbons mix poorly with water. Also, all hydrocarbons are flammable.**

- A **hydrocarbon** is an organic compound that is made up only of carbon and hydrogen. Methane and propane are hydrocarbons.
- Hydrocarbons do not dissolve well in water.
- Hydrocarbons are flammable. They burn very easily.
- The simplest hydrocarbon is methane. The chemical formula for methane is CH_4. The chemical formula shows you that methane has one carbon atom and four hydrogen atoms.
- Propane (C_3H_8) has three carbon atoms and eight hydrogen atoms.

Answer the following questions. Use your textbook and the ideas above.

3. Read each word in the box. In each sentence below, fill in one of the words.

flammable	hydrogen	oxygen	water

a. Hydrocarbons are made up of only the elements carbon and ____________________.

b. Hydrocarbons do not dissolve well in ____________________.

c. Hydrocarbons burn very easily, which means they are ____________________.

4. Fill in the table below about chemical formulas of hydrocarbons.

Hydrocarbons		
Chemical Formula	**Number of Carbon Atoms**	**Number of Hydrogen Atoms**
a. ______	1	4
C_2H_6	**b.** ______	6
C_3H_8	3	**c.** ______

Structure of Hydrocarbons (pages 299–301)

Key Concept: **The carbon chains in a hydrocarbon may be straight, branched, or ring-shaped. In addition to forming a single bond, two carbon atoms can form a double bond or a triple bond.**

- Chemists use structural formulas to show how atoms in a molecule are arranged. A **structural formula** shows the kind, number, and arrangement of atoms in a molecule.
- In a structural formula, a dash shows a bond (C—C).
- Some molecules can be arranged in different ways. Compounds that have the same chemical formula but different structures are called **isomers**. Butane (C_4H_{10}) has two isomers. One isomer is a straight chain. The other isomer is a branched chain. These isomers of butane have different properties.

- Carbon can also form double bonds and triple bonds. In a structural formula, a double bond is shown by a double dash (C═C). A triple bond is shown by a triple dash (C≡C).

Answer the following questions. Use your textbook and the ideas on page 123 and above.

5. In a structural formula, a dash shows a(an) ______________________.

6. This structural formula for propane (C_3H_8) is not complete. Complete this structural formula by showing all the hydrogen atoms that are bonded to the carbon chain.

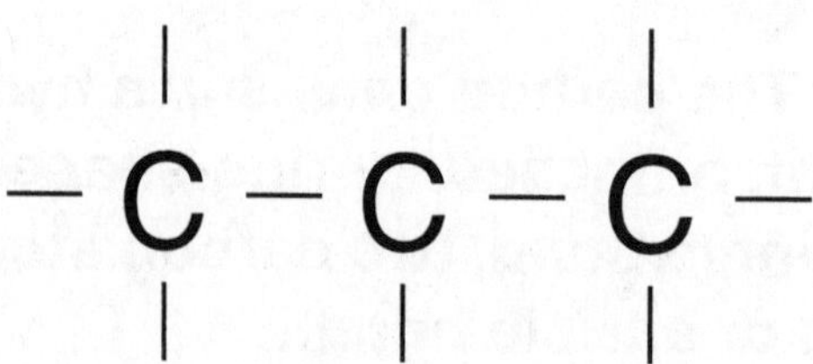

7. Compounds with the same chemical formula but different structures are called ______________________.

Substituted Hydrocarbons (pages 302–303)

Key Concept: **If just one atom of another element is substituted for a hydrogen atom in a hydrocarbon, a different compound is created.**

- In a **substituted hydrocarbon**, atoms of other elements replace one or more hydrogen atoms in the hydrocarbon.
- In some substituted hydrocarbons, one or more halogen atoms replace hydrogen atoms. Elements in the halogen family include fluorine, chlorine, bromine, and iodine.
- A **hydroxyl** (hy DRAHKS il) **group** is made up of an oxygen atom and a hydrogen atom (–OH). A substituted hydrocarbon that has one or more hydroxyl groups in place of a hydrogen is called an **alcohol**.
- An **organic acid** is a substituted hydrocarbon that has one or more carboxyl groups in place of a hydrogen atom. A **carboxyl group** is –COOH. In a carboxyl group, one atom of carbon is bonded to a hydroxyl group (–OH) and double bonded to an oxygen atom.

Answer the following questions. Use your textbook and the ideas above.

8. Read each word in the box. In each sentence below, fill in the correct word or words.

carboxyl group	halogen	hydroxyl group

a. An atom of oxygen bonded to an atom of hydrogen (–OH) is called a ____________________.

b. An atom of carbon bonded to an oxygen atom and a hydroxyl group (–COOH) is called a

____________________.

9. Complete the concept map about substituted hydrocarbons.

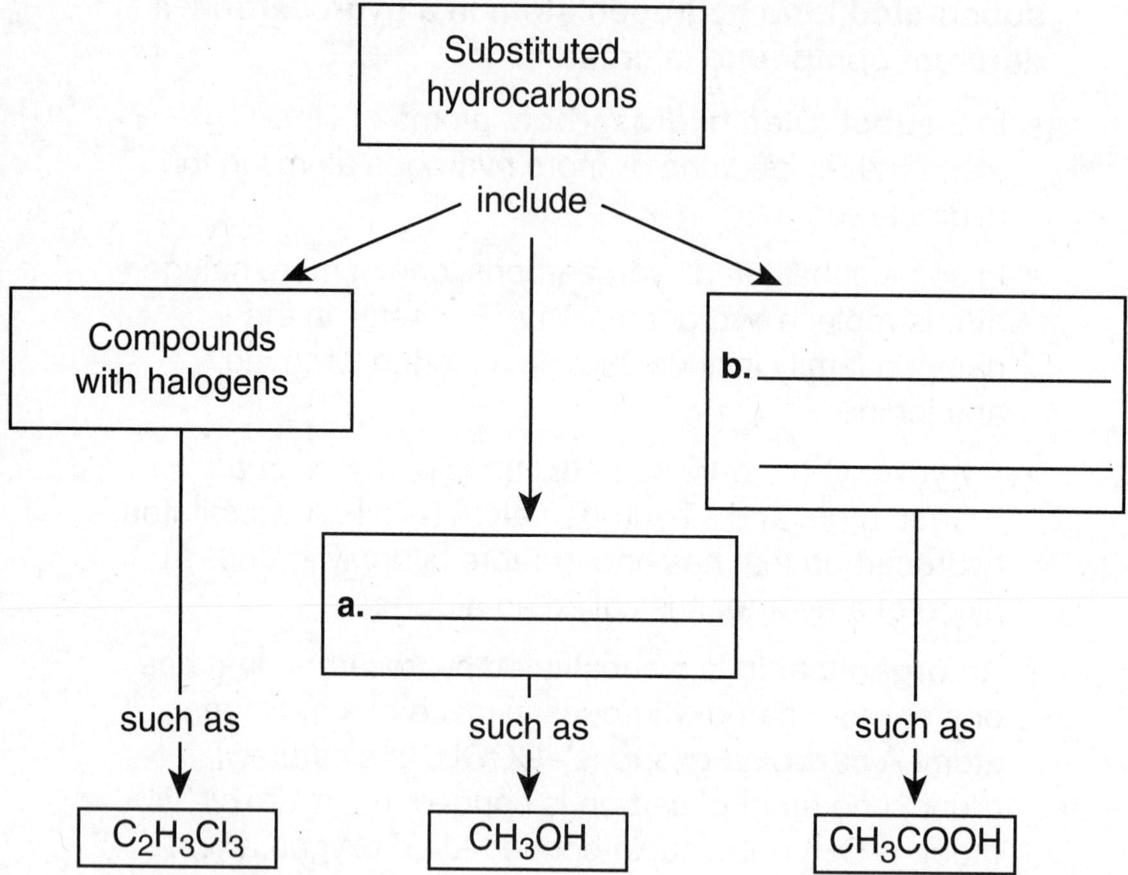

Esters (page 303)

***Key Concept:* Many esters have pleasant, fruity smells.**

- An **ester** is a compound made by chemically combining an alcohol and an organic acid.
- Esters cause the pleasant smell of pineapples, bananas, strawberries, and apples.

Answer the following question. Use your textbook and the ideas on page 126.

10. Circle the letter of each sentence that is true about esters.

a. Esters do not contain an alcohol.

b. An organic acid makes up part of an ester.

c. Esters have a pleasant, fruity smell.

Polymers (page 304)

***Key Concept:* Organic compounds, such as alcohols, esters, and others, can be linked together to build polymers with thousands or even millions of atoms.**

- A **polymer** is a very large molecule made of a chain of many smaller molecules bonded together.
- The small molecules that bond together to build a polymer are called **monomers**.
- Monomers can be alcohols, esters, and other kinds of organic compounds.
- Some polymers are made by living things. Wool, cotton, and silk are natural polymers. Other polymers, such as nylon and plastic, are made by people.

Answer the following questions. Use your textbook and the ideas above.

11. Is the following sentence true or false? A monomer is a very large molecule made of a chain of smaller molecules bonded together. __________

12. Circle the letter of a polymer that is made by people.

a. plastic

b. silk

c. wool

Polymers and Composites

(pages 306–313)

Forming Polymers (page 307)

Key Concept: **Polymers form when chemical bonds link large numbers of monomers in a repeating pattern.**

- A polymer (PAHL uh mur) is a large compound built from smaller compounds in a repeating pattern. Plastic is a polymer. Silk is a polymer, too.
- The small compounds that join to form polymers are called monomers (MAHN uh murz). Polymers can be made of one kind of monomer. Polymers can also be made of two or three monomers joined together in a pattern.
- Polymers are often made of compounds that have the element carbon. Carbon can form many compounds. Carbon atoms can form four chemical bonds. Carbon atoms can join to make compounds with straight chains, branched chains, or rings.

Answer the following questions. Use your textbook and the ideas above.

1. Read each word in the box. In each sentence below, fill in the correct word or words.

monomer	polymer	chemical bond

a. A large compound built from smaller repeating units is a ____________________.

b. A small compound that joins to form larger compounds is a ____________________.

2. Look at the carbon compounds below. Circle the letter of the carbon compound that is a ring.

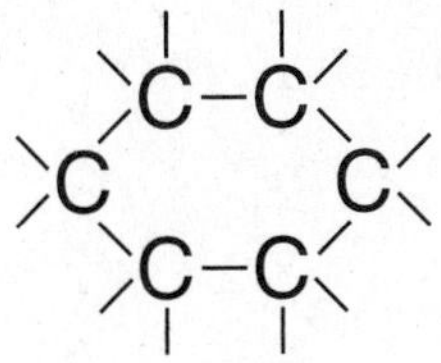

a. 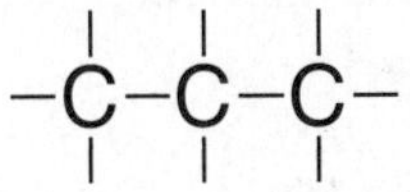 b. 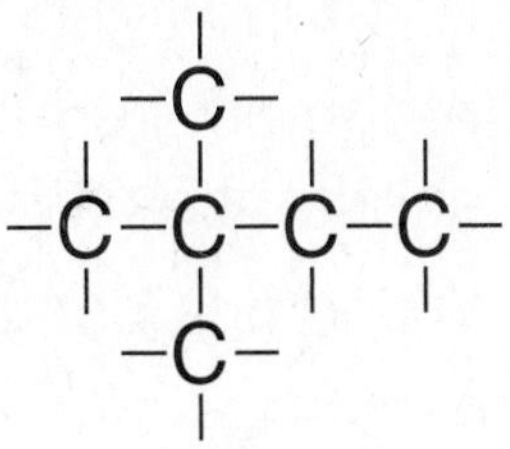 c.

Polymers and Composites (pages 308–312)

***Key Concept:* Many composite materials include one or more polymers.**

- Many plants and animals make polymers. Plants make a polymer called cellulose (SEL yoo lohs).
- Within your body, **proteins** are polymers formed from smaller molecules called amino acids. An **amino acid** is a monomer that is a building block of proteins.
- Many polymers are made by people. **Plastic** is a polymer made by people. It can be molded into different shapes. Carpet and glue are also made of polymers that people have made.
- A **composite** is made of two or more different substances. A composite has different properties than the substances it is made of. Wood is a natural composite. Fiberglass is a composite of glass and plastic.

Answer the following questions. Use your textbook and the ideas above.

3. A protein is a polymer formed from monomers called

a. plastics.

b. cellulose.

c. amino acids.

4. Circle the letter of each sentence that is true about composites.

a. A composite is made from two or more substances.

b. A composite has the same properties as the substances it is made of.

c. Wood is a composite.

Recycling Plastics (pages 312–313)

***Key Concept:* You can help reduce the amount of plastic waste by recycling.**

- Plastics are very useful and cheap to make. Many things are made of plastic. Some grocery bags are plastic. Milk jugs are plastic, too.
- Many plastics are thrown in the trash. Plastics do not break down into simpler materials in the environment. Plastics may last for many years. As a result, plastics increase the amount of trash.
- One way to reduce the amount of plastic trash is to recycle it. Recycled plastics are used to make bottles, clothing, and park benches.

Answer the following questions. Use your textbook and the ideas above.

5. Plastics increase the amount of trash because plastics

a. break down very quickly into simpler materials.

b. do not break down into simpler materials in the environment.

c. do not have very many uses.

6. Is the following sentence true or false? One way to reduce plastic trash is to recycle it. __________

Life With Carbon (pages 316–323)

Carbohydrates (pages 317–318)

Key Concept: **The four classes of organic compounds required by living things are carbohydrates, proteins, lipids, and nucleic acids. The energy released by breaking down starch allows the body to carry out its life functions.**

- A **carbohydrate** is an organic compound made from carbon, hydrogen, and oxygen. Carbohydrates are rich in energy.
- The simplest carbohydrates are sugars. **Glucose** is the most important sugar in your body. The cells in your body use glucose for energy.
- A **complex carbohydrate** is a polymer. Most of the foods you eat are complex carbohydrates.
- **Starch** is a polymer made from glucose. Plants store food in the form of starch. Cereals, rice, and potatoes are foods rich in starch.
- **Cellulose** is another plant polymer made from glucose. Cellulose is part of the stems and roots of plants. Most fruits and vegetables are high in cellulose. Your body, however, cannot break down cellulose to use as energy. Cellulose is an important source of fiber in your diet.

Answer the following questions. Use your textbook and the ideas above.

1. Circle the letter of an organic compound that is made of carbon, hydrogen, and oxygen and is rich in energy.

   a. polymer

   b. carbohydrate

   c. isomer

2. Complete the concept map about carbohydrates.

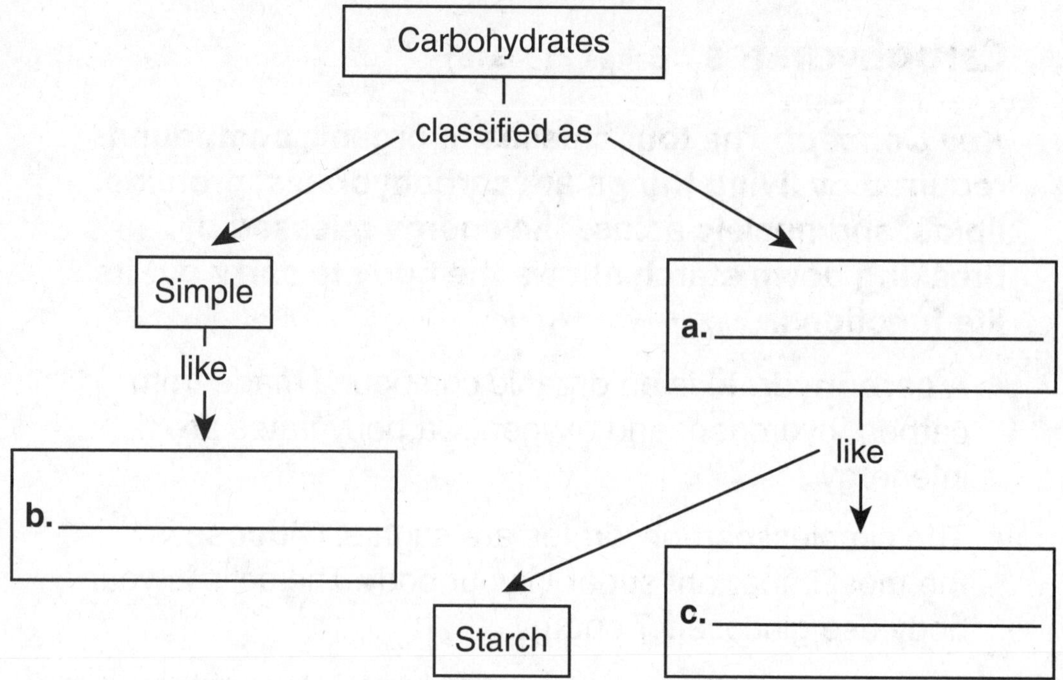

Proteins (page 319)

Key Concept: **The body uses proteins from food to build and repair body parts and to regulate cell activities.**

- **Proteins** are polymers made of smaller molecules called amino acids. Hair, skin, feathers, and spider webs are all made of protein.
- **Amino acids** are monomers that make up proteins. There are 20 different amino acids. Different combinations of amino acids make different proteins.
- Every amino acid has a carboxyl group (–COOH) and an amino group ($-NH_2$).
- Meat, fish, eggs, and milk are foods that have protein. Your body uses protein to build and repair body parts. Proteins also control the chemical reactions that happen in your body.

Answer the following questions. Use your textbook and the ideas on page 132.

3. Read each word in the box. In each sentence below, fill in the correct word or words.

amino acids	carbohydrates	proteins

a. Polymers that make up hair and feathers are called ______________________.

b. Monomers that have a carboxyl group and an amino group are called ______________________.

4. Which is NOT a good source of protein?

a. potatoes

b. meat

c. milk

Lipids (pages 320–321)

***Key Concept:* Gram for gram, lipids release twice as much energy in your body as do carbohydrates.**

- **Lipids** are made of carbon, hydrogen, and oxygen. Lipids are very rich in energy. Lipids release much more energy in your body than do carbohydrates.
- Fats and oils are lipids. Fats are found in foods like meat and butter. Oils are found in foods like peanuts and olives.
- Fats and oils are both made from three fatty acids and one alcohol called glycerol. A **fatty acid** is a monomer of lipids.

Answer the following questions. Use your textbook and the ideas on page 133.

5. Is the following sentence true or false? Lipids release much more energy in your body than do carbohydrates. __________

6. Draw a line from each kind of lipid to its food source. Each lipid may be used more than once.

Lipid	**Food Source**
fat	**a.** meat
	b. peanuts
oil	**c.** butter
	d. olives

Nucleic Acids (pages 321–322)

Key Concept: **When living things reproduce, they pass DNA and the information it carries to the next generation.**

- **Nucleic** (noo KLAY ik) **acids** are very large organic molecules made up of carbon, oxygen, hydrogen, nitrogen, and phosphorus. One kind of nucleic acid is **DNA**, or deoxyribonucleic (dee AHK see ry boh noo klay ik) acid.
- **Nucleotides** (NOO klee oh tydz) are the monomers that join together to make nucleic acids. Only four different nucleotides make up a molecule of DNA.
- The order of nucleotides in a DNA molecule determines the order of amino acids in a protein.

- Different DNA molecules produce different proteins, which cause living things to differ from each other.
- When living things reproduce, they pass DNA molecules to their offspring.

Answer the following questions. Use your textbook and the ideas on page 134 and above.

7. The pictures show two different organic compounds. Circle the letter of the nucleic acid.

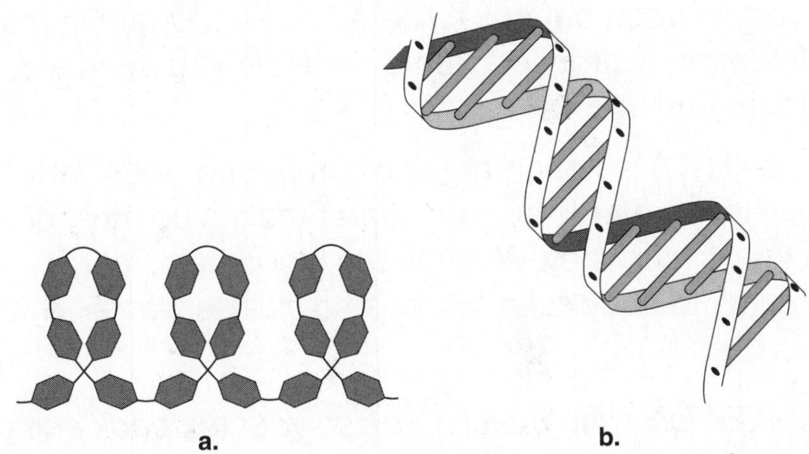

8. Circle the letter of each sentence that is true about nucleic acids.

a. Nucleic acids are made up of amino acids.

b. The order of nucleotides in a DNA molecule determines the order of amino acids in a protein.

c. Living things pass on DNA molecules to their offspring.

Other Nutrients (pages 322–323)

Key Concept: **Organisms require water, vitamins, minerals, and salts to support the functioning of large molecules.**

- Vitamins are organic compounds. Vitamins are molecules that help chemical reactions take place in your body. For example, vitamin C helps keep your skin and gums healthy.
- Minerals are elements in the form of ions. Minerals are not organic compounds. Minerals are important in many different body process. Some minerals you need are calcium and iron.
- Water (H_2O) is not an organic compound. Your body must have water to survive. Water makes up most of the liquids in your body. Water in the blood helps carry nutrients to body cells. Water also carries wastes away from cells.

Answer the following questions. Use your textbook and the ideas above.

9. Is the following sentence true or false? Your body needs vitamins and minerals in only small amounts.

____

10. Draw a line from each term to its meaning.

Term	**Meaning**
vitamins	**a.** elements in the form of ions that help in body processes
minerals	**b.** a compound that makes up most body liquids
water	**c.** organic compounds that help chemical reactions take place in the body

Describing Motion (pages 338–341)

Motion (pages 339–340)

Key Concept: **An object is in motion if it changes position relative to a reference point.**

- **Motion** means moving. To find out if an object is in motion, you must compare it to another object or place. An object is in motion if its distance from another object or place is changing.
- A **reference point** is an object or place that you can use to tell if an object is in motion. A tree, a sign, or a building make good reference points.
- Whether or not an object is in motion depends on the reference point. Suppose you are sitting in a chair. If your chair is your reference point, you are not moving. But if you choose the sun as your reference point, you are moving quite fast. This is because you and your chair are on Earth, which moves around the sun.

Answer the following questions. Use your textbook and the ideas above.

1. Read each word in the box. In each sentence below, fill in the correct word or words.

reference point	force	motion

   a. An object is in ____________________ if its distance from another object or place is changing.

   b. To see if an object is moving, you must compare it to a ____________________.

2. Is the following sentence true or false? Whether or not an object is in motion depends on the reference point.

   ____

Distance and Displacement (pages 340–341)

Key Concept: **Distance is the total length of the actual path between two points. Displacement is the length and direction of a straight line between starting and ending points.**

- When you move, the distance between you and a reference point changes. **Distance** is the length of a path between two points.
- **Displacement** is the length and direction that an object has moved from its starting point.
- A quantity that consists of both a magnitude and a direction is called a **vector**. Displacement is a vector. Distance is not.

Answer the following questions. Use your textbook and the ideas above.

3. Read each word in the box. In each sentence below, fill in the correct word.

distance	vector	displacement

   a. The length and direction of a straight line between starting and ending points is called __________.

   b. When you move, the __________ between you and a reference point changes.

4. Is the following sentence true or false? A measurable quantity that consists of both a magnitude and a direction is called a vector. __________

Speed and Velocity (pages 342–347)

Calculating Speed (pages 342–343)

Key Concept: **To calculate the speed of an object, divide the distance the object travels by the amount of time it takes to travel that distance.**

- **Speed** is a rate. It tells how far something moves in a certain amount of time. For example, *1 meter per second* is a speed.
- To find speed, use the formula:

$$\text{Speed} = \frac{\text{Distance}}{\text{Time}}$$

- On a bike ride, you slow down and speed up. **Average speed** tells the total distance you rode divided by the total time it took. **Instantaneous speed** is the speed you were moving at an instant in time during the bike ride.

Answer the following questions. Use your textbook and the ideas above.

1. Read the words in the box. Use the correct words to fill in the blanks in the formula for speed.

Distance	Rate	Time

Speed = **a.** ______________ / **b.** ______________

2. Is the following sentence true or false? Your average speed on a bike ride was the speed you were moving at an instant in time during the ride. ______________

3. How would you find the speed of a person who walked 10 meters in 8 seconds? Circle the letter of the correct answer.
   a. Speed = 10 meters ÷ 8 seconds
   b. Speed = 8 seconds × 10 meters
   c. Speed = 8 seconds ÷ 10 meters

Velocity (pages 344–346)

Key Concept: **Changes in velocity may be due to changes in speed, changes in direction, or both.**

- **Velocity** is speed in a given direction.
- For example, the velocity of a person walking is 3 kilometers per hour, west. This tells the speed the person is walking. It also tells you the direction the person is walking.

Answer the following questions. Use your textbook and the ideas above.

4. Speed in a given direction is ____________________.

5. What do you need to know to describe the velocity of an object? Circle the letter of each thing you need to know.
   a. distance
   b. direction
   c. speed

6. A velocity tells speed and direction. Circle the letter of each velocity.
   a. 2 meters per second east
   b. 5 kilometers per hour
   c. 10 meters per second west

Graphing Speed (pages 346–347)

***Key Concept:* The slope of a distance-versus-time graph represents speed, that is, the rate that distance changes in relation to time.**

- Motion can be shown on a line graph. A motion graph shows time along the bottom, or *x*-axis. A motion graph shows distance along the side, or *y*-axis.
- The steepness of the line on the graph is called **slope**. A line that rises steeply shows that an object is moving quickly. A line that rises less steeply shows that an object is moving more slowly. A line that is flat shows that an object is not moving at all.

Answer the following questions. Use your textbook and the ideas above.

7. The steepness of the line on a graph is called

______________________.

8. Look at the graph. Which part of the line shows a time when the object was not moving?

a. A

b. B

c. C

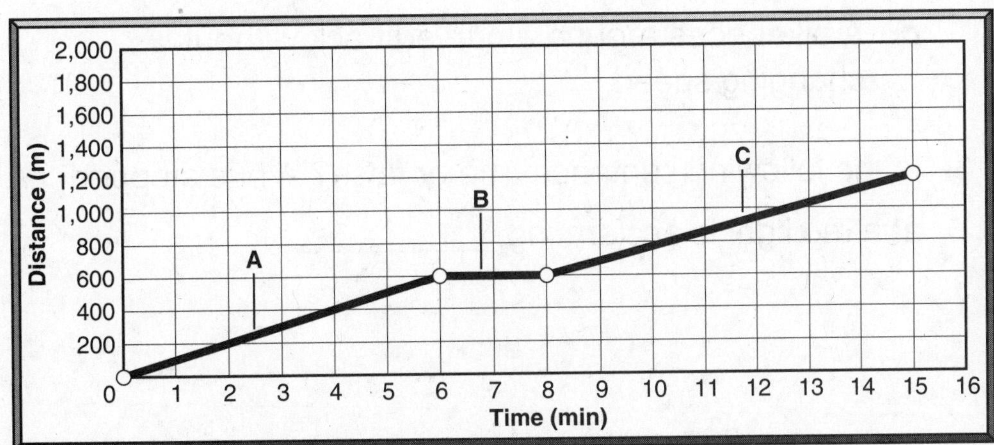

Acceleration (pages 350–355)

Changing Velocity (pages 350–351)

Key Concept: **In science, acceleration refers to increasing speed, decreasing speed, or changing direction.**

- Remember that velocity is speed and direction. **Acceleration** is the rate at which velocity changes.
- Objects accelerate when they speed up. A car that goes faster is accelerating.
- Objects accelerate when they slow down. A rolling ball that slows down is accelerating.
- Objects accelerate when they change direction. A bus that turns a corner is accelerating.

Answer the following questions. Use your textbook and the ideas above.

1. The rate at which velocity changes is

   ______________________.

2. Circle the letter of each example of acceleration.
   - **a.** A ball speeds up as it rolls down a hill.
   - **b.** A car slows down as it comes to a stop sign.
   - **c.** A biker goes around a curved track without changing speed.

3. Is the following sentence true or false? A bus stopped at a red light is acclerating. __________

Calculating Acceleration (pages 352–353)

Key Concept: **To determine the acceleration of an object, you must calculate its change in velocity per unit of time.**

- To find acceleration, you need to know three things:
  1. You need to know the starting velocity.
  2. You need to know the ending velocity.
  3. You need to know how long it took for the object to change velocities.
- The formula for acceleration is:

$$\text{Acceleration} = \frac{\text{Final velocity} - \text{Initial velocity}}{\text{Time}}$$

- The unit for acceleration is meters per second per second, or m/s^2.

Answer the following questions. Use your textbook and the ideas above.

4. Read the words in the box. Use the words to fill in the blanks in the formula for acceleration.

Final velocity	Time	Distance

$$\text{Acceleration} = \frac{\textbf{a.}\ \_\_\_\_\_\_\_\_\_\_ - \text{Initial velocity}}{\textbf{b.}\ \_\_\_\_\_\_\_\_\_\_}$$

5. Is the following sentence true or false? Acceleration is measured in meters per second per second.

____

6. A student used this formula to find the acceleration of an object:

$$\frac{8\ \text{m/s} - 2\ \text{m/s}}{3\ \text{s}} =$$

a. What is the final velocity of the object?

____

b. What is the initial velocity of the object?

____

c. How long did it take the object to change velocities? ______________________

Graphing Acceleration (pages 354–355)

Key Concept: **You can use both a speed-versus-time graph and a distance-versus-time graph to analyze the motion of an accelerating object.**

- Acceleration can be shown on a line graph.
- A speed-versus-time graph shows time on the bottom, or *x*-axis. It shows speed on the side, or *y*-axis. A straight, slanted line on this kind of graph shows acceleration.
- A distance-versus-time graph shows time on the *x*-axis. It shows distance on the *y*-axis. A curved line on this kind of graph shows acceleration.

Answer the following questions. Use your textbook and the ideas above.

7. Circle the letter of the kind of graph that can be used to show acceleration.

a. circle graph

b. bar graph

c. line graph

8. Fill in blanks in the table about acceleration graphs.

Acceleration Graphs	
Type of Graph	**Acceleration Is Shown as**
a. ______________	straight, slanted line
b. ______________	curved line

9. Use the graphs to answer the questions.

Graph A

Speed (m/s)
0 3 6 9 12 15 18 21 24
0 1 2 3 4
Time (s)

Graph B

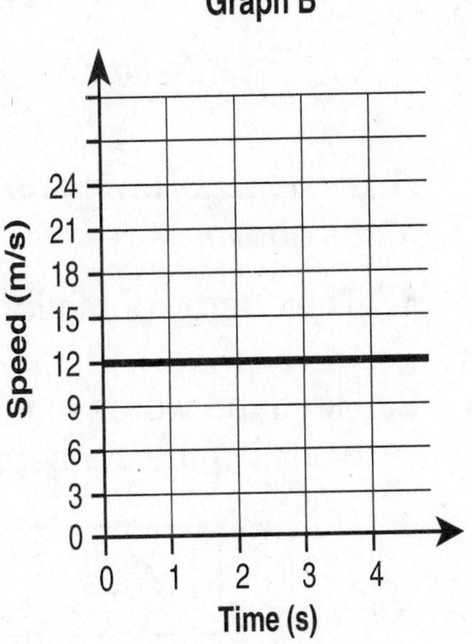

a. Which graph shows an object that is moving at a steady speed? ______________

b. Which graph shows an object with a changing speed? ______________

c. Which graph shows acceleration?

____

Energy (pages 358–363)

Kinetic Energy (page 359)

***Key Concept:* The kinetic energy of an object depends on both its mass and its speed.**

- When a force moves an object, **work** is done. **Energy** is the ability to do work.
- **Kinetic energy** is energy of motion.
- The faster an object moves, the more kinetic energy it has. The more mass an object has, the more kinetic energy it has.
- There is a mathematical relationship between kinetic energy, mass, and speed.

$$\text{Kinetic energy} = \frac{1}{2} \times \text{mass} \times \text{speed}^2$$

Answer the following questions. Use your textbook and the ideas above.

1. The energy of motion is called ____________________.

2. Read the words in the box. Use the words to fill in the blanks in the concept map about kinetic energy.

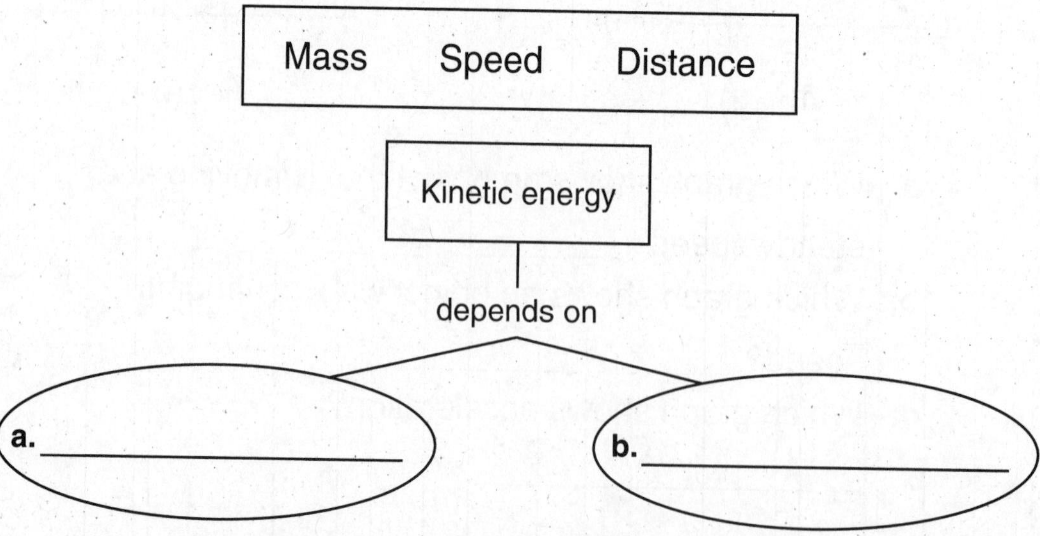

Potential Energy (page 360)

Key Concept: **An object's gravitational potential energy depends on its weight and on its height relative to a reference point.**

- **Potential energy** is stored energy. Energy can be stored in an object because of where it is or because of its shape.
- A book sitting on a desk has potential energy. Energy was stored in the book when it was lifted onto the desk. Potential energy due to an object's height is called **gravitational potential energy**. The greater an object's height, the more gravitational potential energy it has. The greater an object's weight, the more gravitational potential energy it has.
- **Elastic potential energy** is the energy in springs and archery bows.

Answer the following questions. Use your textbook and the ideas above.

3. Stored energy is called ____________________.

4. Read each word in the box. In each sentence below, fill in the correct word or words.

gravitational potential	kinetic
elastic potential	

a. A stretched rubber band has ____________________________ energy.

b. A book on top of a desk has ____________________________ energy.

Energy Transformation and Conservation (pages 361–363)

Key Concept: **Any object that rises or falls experiences a change in its kinetic and gravitational energy. According to the law of conservation of energy, energy cannot be created or destroyed.**

- Energy can change forms. An **energy transformation** is a change from one form of energy to another form of energy.
- **Mechanical energy** is the energy an object has because of its position and its motion.
- You can find an object's mechanical energy by adding its kinetic energy and its potential energy. Use this formula:

$$\text{Mechanical energy} = \text{Potential energy} + \text{Kinetic energy}$$

- Energy changes form when an object moves up or down. The object has the most potential energy at its highest point. The object has the most kinetic energy at its lowest point.
- A pendulum changes energy as it swings. It has the most potential energy at its highest point. It has the most kinetic energy at its lowest point.
- The amount of energy does not change when energy changes forms. Energy is not lost. Energy is not created. This is the **law of conservation of energy**.

Answer the following questions. Use your textbook and the ideas above.

5. Is this sentence true or false? Energy never changes forms. __________

6. Circle the letter of the formula for mechanical energy.
   a. Mechanical energy = Potential energy − Kinetic energy
   b. Mechanical energy = Potential energy + Kinetic energy
   c. Mechanical energy = Potential energy × Kinetic energy

Use the picture to answer questions 7 and 8.

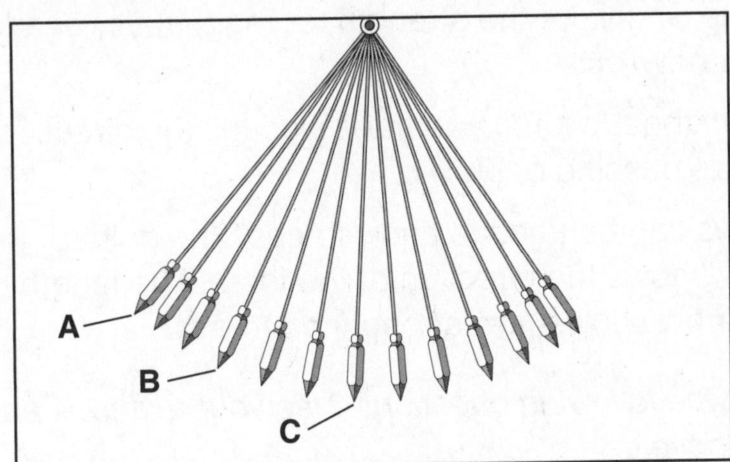

7. At what point does the pendulum have the greatest potential energy? __________

8. At what point does the pendulum have the greatest kinetic energy? __________

9. Is the following sentence true or false? Energy can be destroyed, but energy cannot be created.

   ____

The Nature of Force (pages 374–377)

What Is a Force? (pages 374–375)

Key Concept: **A force is described by its magnitude and by the direction in which it acts.**

- A **force** is a push or a pull.
- To tell about a force, you must tell how strong the force is. The SI unit for the strength, or magnitude, of a force is the **newton**.
- To tell about a force you must also tell the direction the force is pushing or pulling.
- Arrows can be used to show forces. The point of the arrow shows the direction of the force. The length of the arrow shows how strong the force is.

Answer the following questions. Use your textbook and the ideas above.

1. Circle the letter of the arrow that shows the force with greater strength, or magnitude.

a. **b.**

2. Is the following sentence true or false? Forces are described by their magnitude and their direction.

____

3. The SI unit used for measuring the strength of a force is the ____________________.

4. Read the words in the box. Use the words to fill in the concept map about force.

Magnitude	Distance	Direction

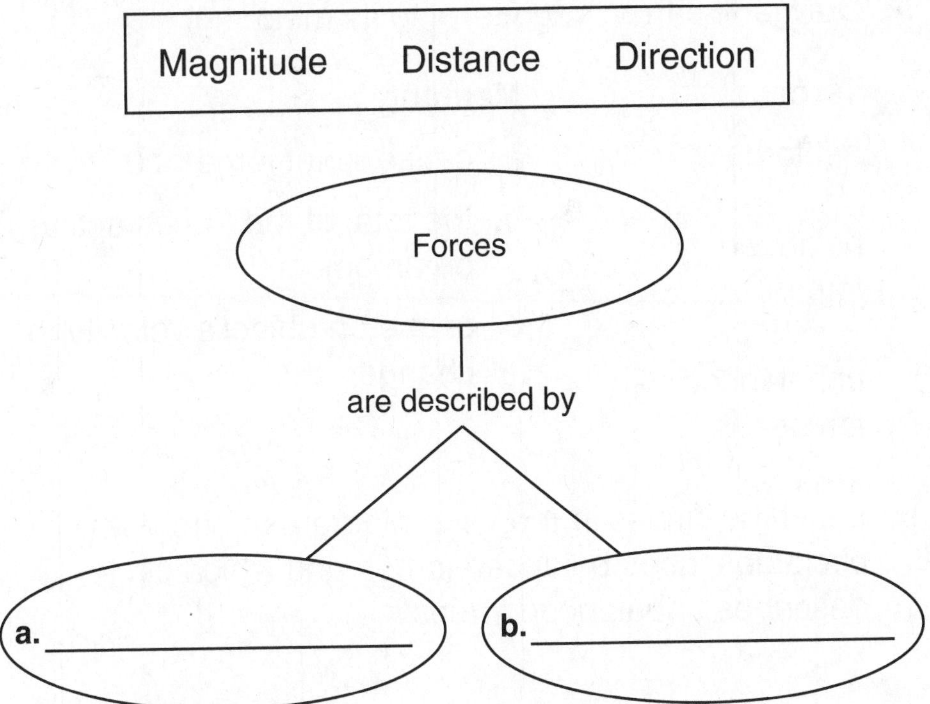

Combining Forces (pages 375–377)

***Key Concept:* Unbalanced forces acting on an object result in a net force and cause a change in the object's velocity. Balanced forces acting on an object do not change the object's velocity.**

- Often there is more than one force acting on an object. The combination of all the forces acting on an object is called the **net force**.
- Sometimes the net force on an object is 0. This means there are **balanced forces** acting on the object. The object's velocity does not change.
- Sometimes the net force does not equal 0. This means there are **unbalanced forces** acting on the object. The object's velocity changes.

Answer the following questions. Use your textbook and the ideas on page 151.

5. Draw a line from each term to its meaning.

Term	**Meaning**
net force	**a.** cause a net force of 0
balanced forces	**b.** the total of the forces acting on an object
unbalanced forces	**c.** cause an object's velocity to change

6. Label the circles in the Venn diagram to show which circle describes balanced forces and which circle describes unbalanced forces.

a. _______________ **b.** _______________

_______________ _______________

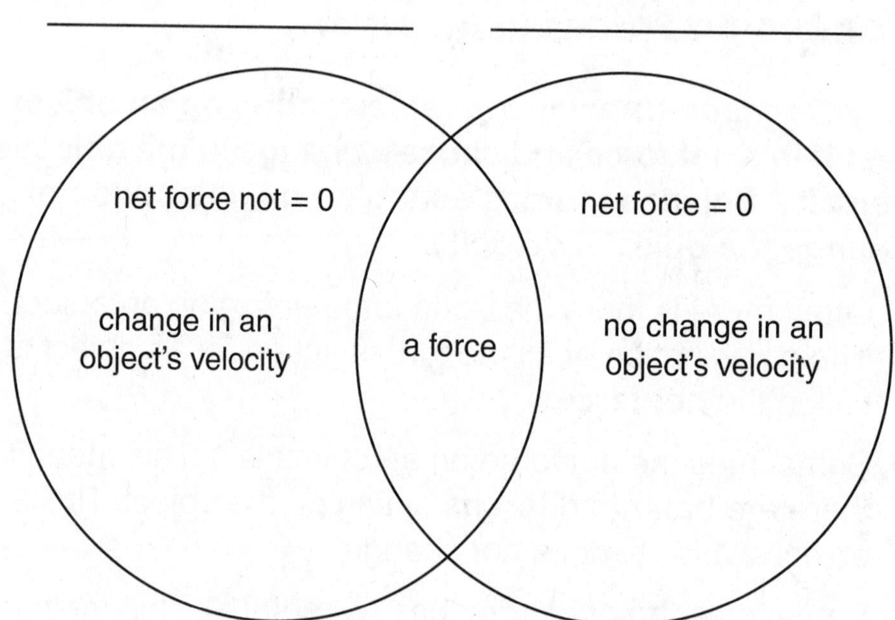

Friction, Gravity, and Elastic Forces (pages 380–388)

Friction (pages 381–383)

Key Concept: **The strength of the force of friction depends on the types of surfaces involved and on how hard the surfaces push together.**

- **Friction** is a force caused by two objects rubbing together. Friction acts in a direction opposite the direction of the moving object.
- The amount of friction depends on two things: how smooth the objects are and how hard they push together.
- There are four kinds of friction:
  1. **Static friction** acts on objects that are not moving.
  2. **Sliding friction** happens when two solid surfaces slide past each other.
  3. **Rolling friction** occurs when an object rolls across a surface.
  4. **Fluid friction** happens when a solid moves through a fluid, like water or air.

Answer the following questions. Use your textbook and the ideas above.

1. A force caused by two objects rubbing together is

______________________.

2. Circle the letter of each true sentence about friction.

a. Friction acts in the same direction as motion.

b. There are four kinds of friction.

c. The amount of friction depends only on how smooth the objects are.

3. Friction acts in a direction opposite the direction of the moving ______________________.

4. Read the words in the box. Use the words to fill in the blanks in the table about friction.

Static friction	Fluid friction	Sliding friction

Friction	
Kind of Friction	**Friction Occurs When...**
Rolling friction	an object rolls across a surface
a. ______________________	an object moves through air or water
b. ______________________	one object slides over another
c. ______________________	objects are not moving

Gravity (pages 384–385)

Key Concept: **The force of gravity between objects increases with greater mass and decreases with greater distance.**

- **Gravity** is a force that pulls objects toward each other.
- Gravity depends on mass. **Mass** is how much matter is in an object.

- Gravity depends on distance. As the distance between objects increases, the force of gravity decreases.
- **Weight** measures the force of gravity on an object at the surface of a planet. An object's weight can change if the force of gravity changes.

Answer the following questions. Use your textbook and the ideas above and on page 154.

5. A force that pulls objects toward each other is

______________________.

6. Read each word in the box. In each sentence below, fill in the correct word or words.

increases	decreases	stays the same

a. If two objects move farther apart, the force of gravity between them ______________________.

b. An object's mass ______________________ if less gravity acts on the object.

7. What is weight? Circle the letter of the correct answer.

a. a force that pulls objects toward each other

b. the amount of matter in an object

c. the force of gravity on an object at a planet's surface

Gravity and Motion (pages 386–387)

Key Concept: **In free fall, the force of gravity alone causes an object to accelerate in the downward direction.**

- Gravity is the force that pulls objects toward Earth.
- If gravity is the only force pulling on an object, the object is in **free fall**.

- Most objects move through air. Fluid friction caused by air is called **air resistance**. Air resistance is a force that pushes upward on falling objects.
- An object that is thrown is called a **projectile**.

Elastic Forces (page 388)

***Key Concept:* Matter is considered elastic if it returns to its original shape after it is squeezed or stretched.**

- **Compression** is an elastic force that squeezes matter. **Tension** is an elastic force that stretches matter.

Answer the following questions. Use your textbook and the ideas above and on page 155.

8. Read the words in the box. Use the correct words to label the forces in the picture.

Gravity	Projectile	Air resistance

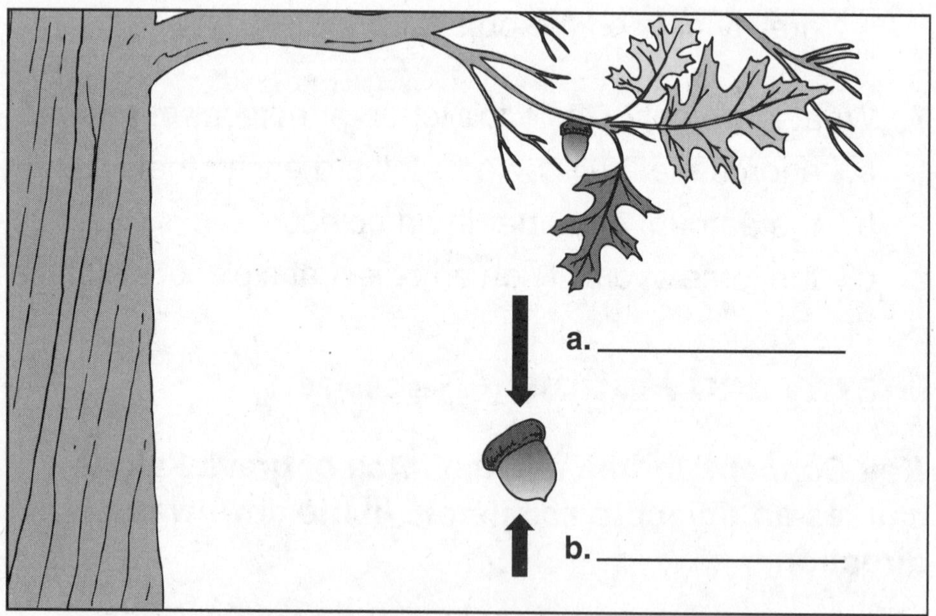

9. Stretching a rubber band uses the elastic force called

______________.

Newton's First and Second Laws (pages 389–392)

The First Law of Motion (pages 389–390)

Key Concept: **Newton's first law of motion states that an object will remain at rest or move at a constant velocity, unless it is acted upon by an unbalanced force.**

- Isaac Newton studied motion in the 1600s.
- Newton's first law of motion says that a moving object will not speed up, slow down, or stop unless it is acted on by an unbalanced force. It also says that an object that is not moving will not start moving unless it is acted on by an unbalanced force.
- Objects resist a change in motion. This is called **inertia** (in UR shuh). All objects have inertia. The greater the mass of an object is, the greater its inertia.

Answer the following questions. Use your textbook and the ideas above.

1. Look at the two pictures. Circle the letter of the picture that shows the object with greater inertia.

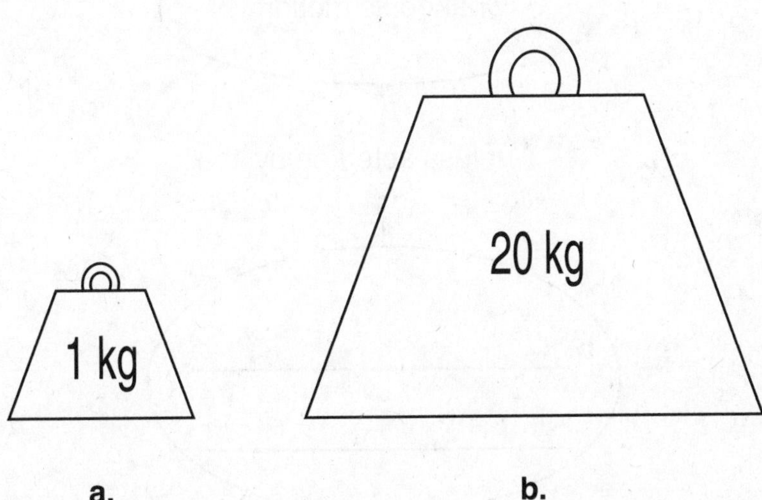

a. **b.**

2. Read the words in the box. Use the correct words to fill in the blanks in the concept map about Newton's first law.

A moving object	Inertia	An unbalanced force

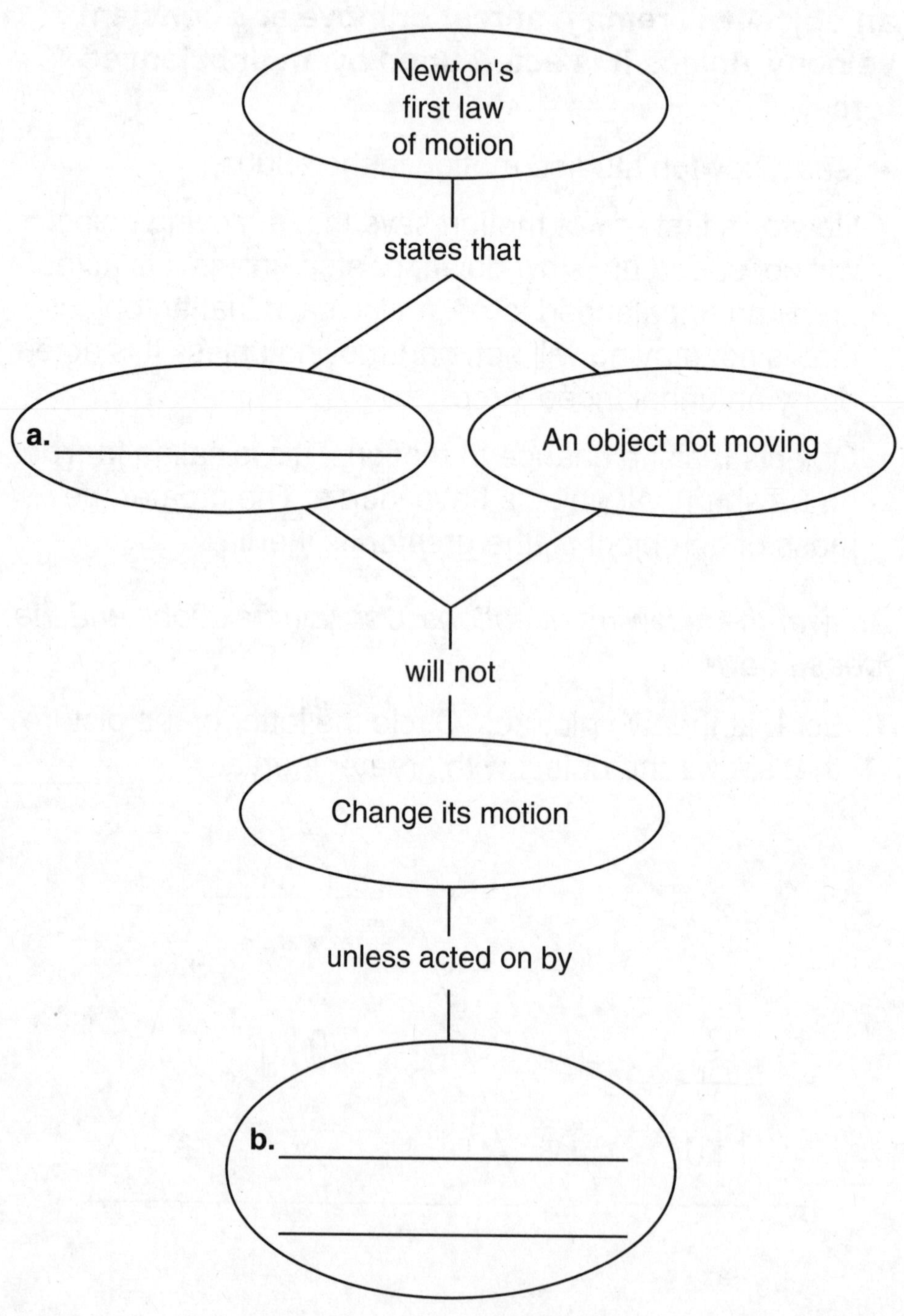

The Second Law of Motion (pages 390–392)

***Key Concept:* Newton's second law of motion states that acceleration depends on the net force acting on the object and on the object's mass.**

- An unbalanced force changes an object's motion. Changing motion is acceleration.
- Newton's second law of motion says that an object's acceleration depends on two things: the net force and the mass of the object.
- Newton's second law can be shown as a formula:

$$\text{Acceleration} = \frac{\text{Net Force}}{\text{Mass}}$$

Answer the following questions. Use your textbook and the ideas above.

3. Is this sentence true or false? An object's acceleration depends on its mass and the net force acting on it. __________

4. A student used this formula to find the acceleration of an object:

$$\text{Acceleration} = \frac{15\text{ N}}{5\text{ kg}}$$

a. How much net force is acting on the object?

____

b. What is the object's mass? ____________________

c. What is the object's acceleration? Show your work below. ____________________ m/s^2

Newton's Third Law (pages 393–399)

Newton's Third Law of Motion (pages 393–395)

Key Concept: **Newton's third law of motion states that if one object exerts a force on another object, then the second object exerts a force of equal strength in the opposite direction on the first object.**

- Newton's third law of motion says that forces come in pairs. When one object exerts a force on a second object, the second object exerts a force back on the first object. The forces are of equal strength. The forces are opposite in direction.
- These two forces are called action force and reaction force. When you jump, the action force is your feet pushing down on the ground. The reaction force is the ground pushing back on your feet.

Answer the following question. Use your textbook and the ideas above.

1. Read the words in the box. Use the correct words to fill in the blanks in the concept map about action and reaction forces.

Equal	Opposite	Unequal

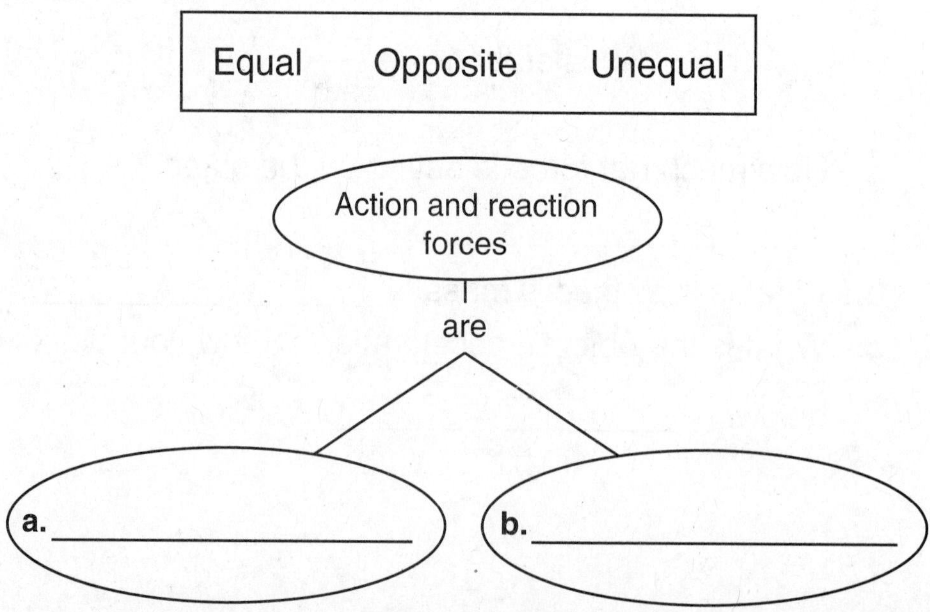

Momentum (pages 396–397)

***Key Concept:* You can calculate the momentum of a moving object by multiplying the object's mass and velocity.**

- The **momentum** (moh MEN tum) of a moving object is its mass times its velocity.
- Momentum has an amount and a direction. The unit for momentum is kg·m/s.
- An object with a large mass or a fast velocity has a large amount of momentum. The more momentum an object has, the harder it is to stop.
- A speeding truck has a large amount of momentum. A small car moving at the same velocity has less momentum than the truck.

Answer the following questions. Use your textbook and the ideas above.

2. Read the words in the box. Use the words to fill in the blanks in the formula for momentum.

Mass	Velocity	Acceleration

Momentum = **a.** ______________ × **b.** ______________

3. Circle the letter of the object with the greatest momentum.

a. a person walking at 2 m/s

b. a car moving at 20 m/s

c. a mouse walking at 0.2 m/s

Conservation of Momentum (pages 397–399)

Key Concept: **The total momentum of any group of objects remains the same, or is conserved, unless outside forces act on the objects.**

- Moving objects sometimes bump one another. When that happens, some momentum can move from one object to another. However, the total momentum stays the same. This is the law of **conservation of momentum**.
- When one moving object hits an object that is moving at a different velocity, some momentum is passed on, or transferred.
- When a moving object hits an object that is not moving, all of the momentum is transferred to the object that was not moving.

Answer the following questions. Use your textbook and the ideas above.

4. Look at the picture. What is the total momentum of the two train cars *after* they collide? ______________________

Before

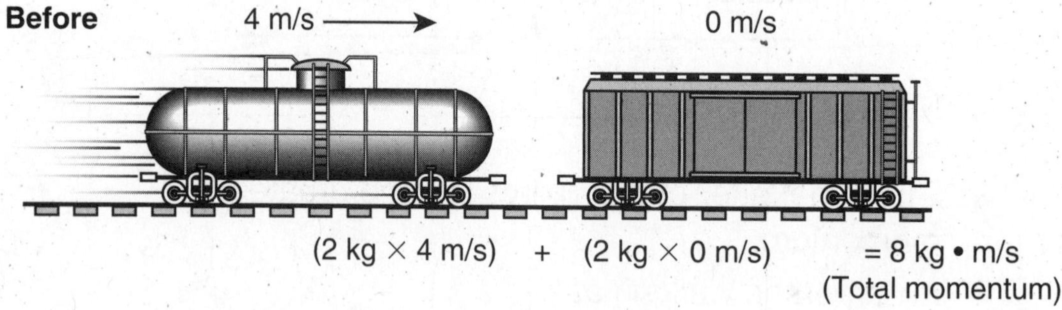

After

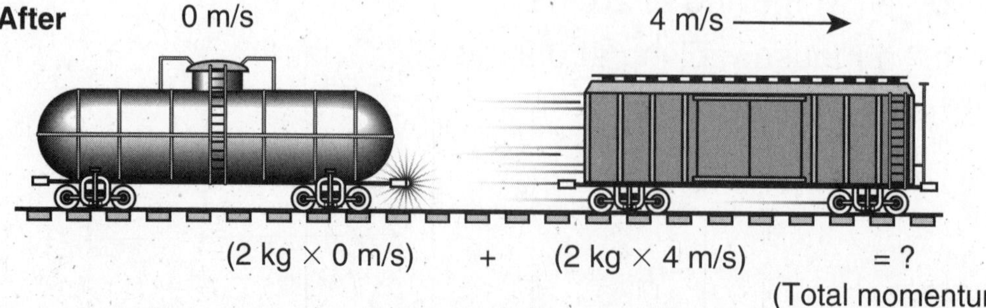

5. Read the words in the box. Use the correct words to fill in the blanks in the concept map about the conservation of momentum.

Momentum	Velocity	Lost

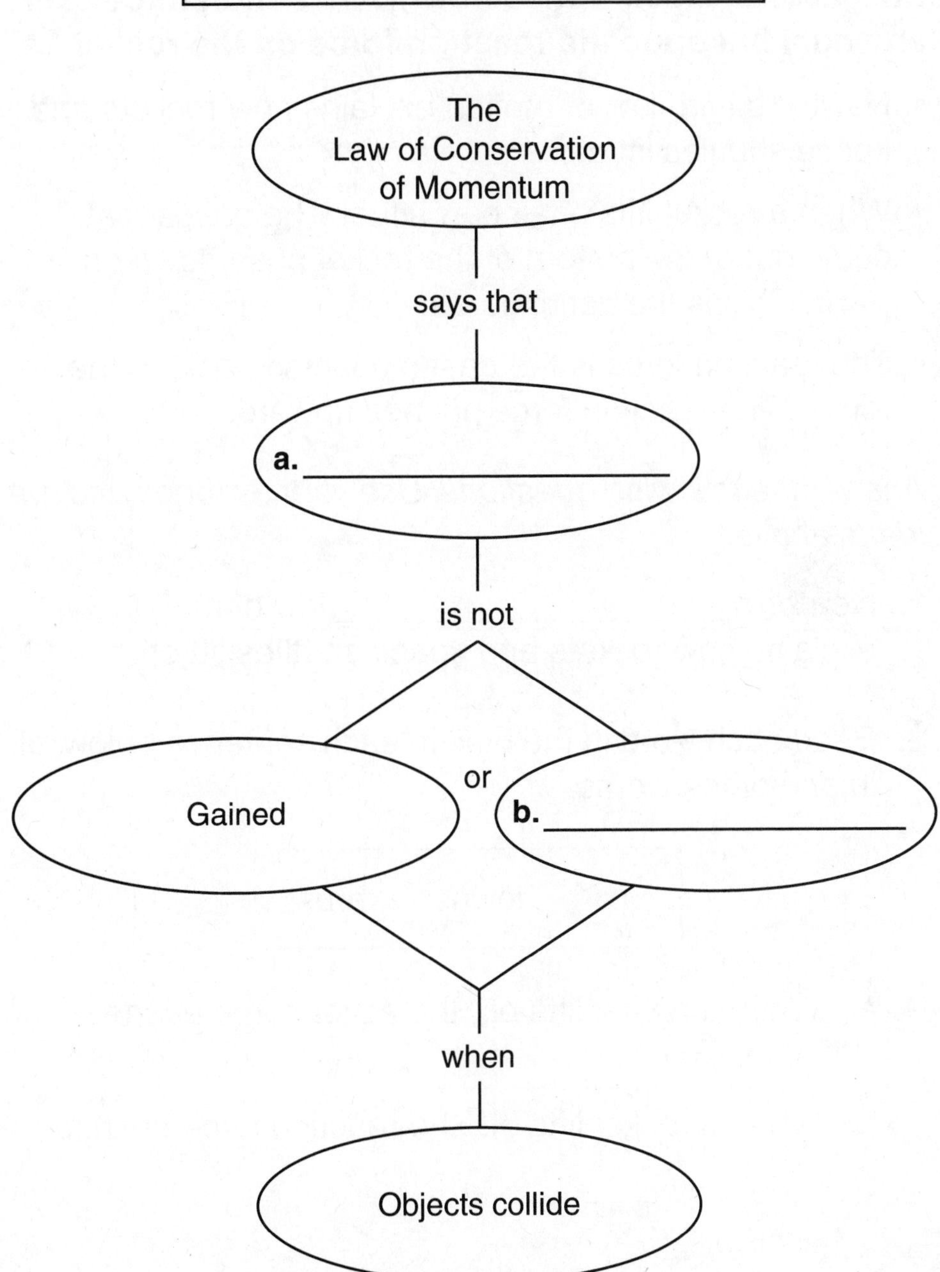

Rockets and Satellites (pages 402–405)

How Do Rockets Lift Off? (page 403)

Key Concept: **A rocket can rise into the air because the gases it expels with a downward action force exert an equal but opposite reaction force on the rocket.**

- Newton's third law of motion explains how rockets and space shuttles lift off.
- When a rocket lifts off, it burns fuel. The gases that come out of the bottom of the rocket push down on Earth. This is the action force.
- The reaction force is the gases pushing back on the rocket. The reaction force pushes upward.

Answer the following questions. Use your textbook and the ideas above.

1. Newton's ____________________ law of motion explains how rockets and space shuttles lift off.

2. Read each word in the box. In each sentence below, fill in one of the words.

up	down	thrust

a. When a rocket lifts off, the action force pushes

____________________.

b. When a rocket lifts off, the reaction force pushes

____________________.

3. Read the words in the box. Use the words to label the picture of the space shuttle lifting off.

Action force	Reaction force

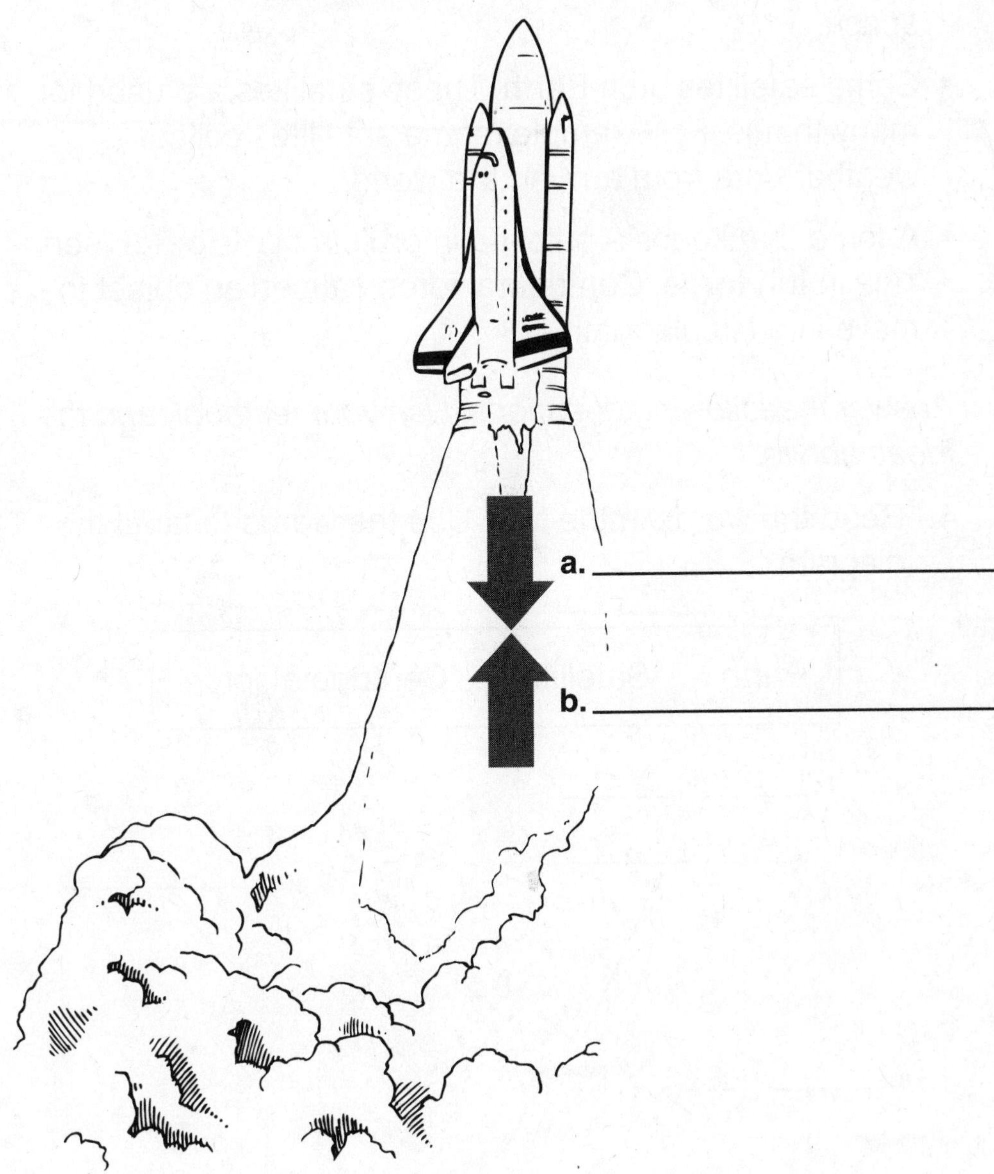

What Is a Satellite? (pages 403–405)

***Key Concept:* Satellites in orbit around Earth continuously fall toward Earth, but because Earth is curved they travel around it.**

- A **satellite** orbits, or moves around, another object in space.
- Some satellites orbit Earth. These satellites are used for many things. For example, some satellites collect weather data from around the world.
- A force that keeps a satellite in orbit is **centripetal** (sen TRIP ih tul) **force**. Centripetal force causes an object to move in a circular path.

Answer the following questions. Use your textbook and the ideas above.

4. Read the words in the box. Use the words to label the diagram.

Earth	Satellite	Centripetal force

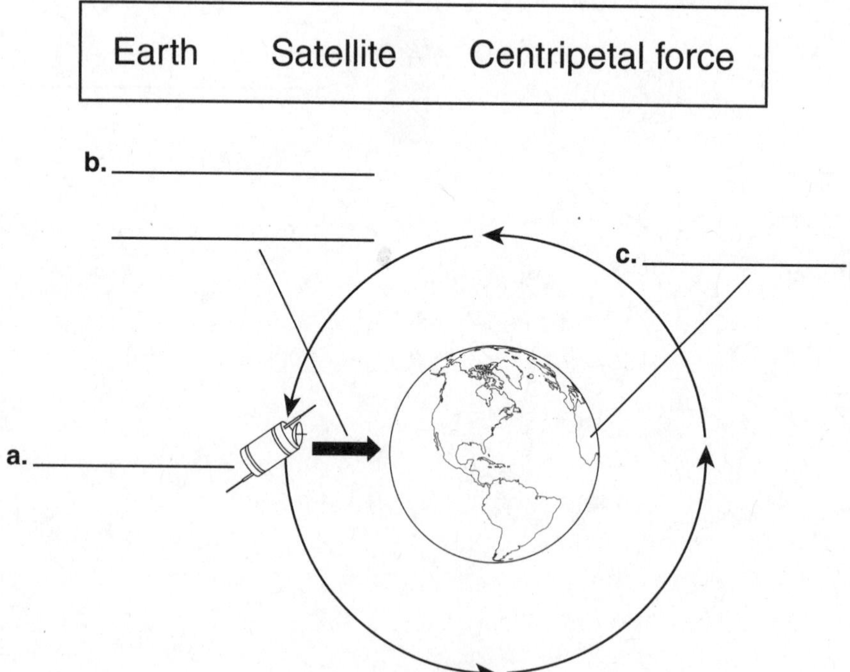

5. The force that keeps a satellite in orbit is

______________________.

Pressure (pages 416–422)

What Is Pressure? (pages 416–417)

***Key Concept:* The amount of pressure you exert depends on the area over which you exert a force.**

- **Pressure** tells how much force pushes on each part of a surface.
- The formula for pressure is:

$$\text{Pressure} = \frac{\text{Force}}{\text{Area}}$$

- The unit for pressure is called the **pascal** (Pa).

Answer the following questions. Use your textbook and the ideas above.

1. Read each word in the box. In each sentence below, fill in one of the words.

force	area	pascal

   a. The unit for pressure is called the ______________________.

   b. Pressure is ______________________ divided by area.

2. Circle the letter of each sentence that is true about pressure.
   a. Pressure cannot be measured.
   b. The unit for pressure is called the pascal.
   c. Pressure tells how much force pushes on each part of a surface.

Fluid Pressure (pages 418–419)

***Key Concept:* In a fluid, all of the forces exerted by the individual particles combine to make up the pressure exerted by the fluid.**

- A **fluid** is a material that can easily flow such as air, a gas, or water, a liquid.
- The tiny particles in a fluid constantly move in all directions. The particles collide with each other and with any surface they meet. Fluid pressure is the force exerted by the particles of a fluid.
- Air is a fluid. Air pushes down on everything on Earth. Air pressure is one kind of fluid pressure.

Answer the following questions. Use your textbook and the ideas above.

3. Read each word in the box. In each sentence below, fill in one of the words.

fluid	particles	air pressure

a. A liquid or a gas is a(an) ____________________.

b. All liquids and gases are made up of ____________________.

4. The force exerted by the particles of a fluid is called ____________________.

5. Is the following sentence true or false? Air pressure is one kind of fluid pressure. __________

Name ______________________ Date ______________ Class ____________

Variations in Fluid Pressure (pages 420–422)

Key Concept: **Atmospheric pressure decreases as your elevation increases. Water pressure increases as depth increases.**

- There are different amounts of air pressure in different places. There is less air pressure in high places, such as on a mountain top. There is more air pressure in lower places, such as in a valley.
- Water also exerts fluid pressure. The deeper you go in the water, the more water pressure pushes on you.
- Air pressure is measured with a **barometer**.

Answer the following questions. Use your textbook and the ideas above.

Use the picture to answer questions 6 and 7.

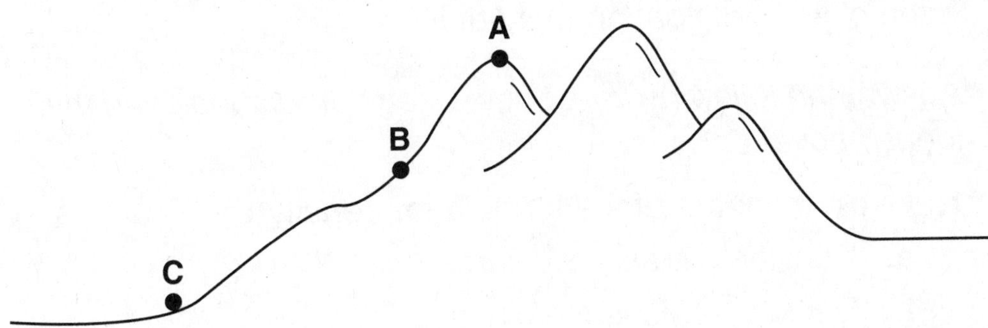

6. At which place is pressure the greatest? __________

7. At which place is there the least pressure? __________

8. Circle the letter of the tool that is used to measure air pressure.

a. thermometer

b. barometer

c. graduated cylinder

Floating and Sinking (pages 424–429)

Density (pages 425–426)

Key Concept: **By comparing densities, you can predict whether an object will float or sink in a fluid.**

- **Density** tells how much mass an object has for its volume. Wood does not have much mass for its volume. Wood has a low density. Mercury has more mass for its volume. Mercury has a greater density than wood.
- To find density, you can use the formula:

$$\text{Density} = \frac{\text{Mass}}{\text{Volume}}$$

- If an object is more dense than a fluid, the object will sink in that fluid. If an object is less dense than a fluid, the object will float on that fluid.

Answer the following questions. Use your textbook and the ideas above.

1. Circle the letter of the formula for density.

a. Density = Mass + Volume

b. Density = Mass × Volume

c. Density = Mass ÷ Volume

2. Fill in the blanks in the table about density.

Density	
Object's Density	**What Object Does**
More dense than fluid	**a.** ____________________
Less dense than fluid	**b.** ____________________

3. The pictures show two objects in water. Both objects have the same volume. Write the letter of the correct sentence under each picture.

a. Object is more dense than water.

b. Object is less dense than water.

c. Object has a density equal to water's density.

__________ __________

Buoyancy (page 427)

Key Concept: **The buoyant force acts in the direction opposite to the force of gravity, so it makes an object feel lighter.**

- Water and other fluids push up on objects. This upward push is called the **buoyant force**. It makes objects in fluid feel lighter.
- If an object's weight is more than the buoyant force, the object will sink. If an object's weight is equal to the buoyant force, the object will float.

Answer the following questions. Use your textbook and the ideas on page 171.

4. The upward push of a fluid on an object is called the ______________________.

5. Circle the letter of each sentence that is true about buoyant force.

a. It pushes upward.

b. It makes objects feel lighter.

c. It pushes downward.

6. Read each word in the box. Use the words to fill in the blanks in the table about buoyancy.

sinks	floats

Buoyancy	
Object's Weight	**What the Object Does**
More than the buoyant force	**a.** ______________________
Equal to the buoyant force	**b.** ______________________

Archimedes' Principle (pages 428–429)

The buoyant force acting on an object in a fluid is equal to the weight of the fluid displaced by the object.

- When an object is placed in a fluid, it takes up space. Some of the fluid needs to move to make room for the object. The weight of the fluid that needs to move is equal to the buoyant force. This idea is **Archimedes' principle**.
- A big object takes up more room than a small object. So a big object is acted on by a greater buoyant force than a small object.

Answer the following questions. Use your textbook and the ideas above.

7. Circle the letter of what the buoyant force on an object is equal to.

  a. the weight of the object

  b. the weight of the fluid the object moves

  c. the weight of the air pressing on the object

8. Is the following sentence true of false? A boat floats because the bouyant force acting on the boat is less than the weight of the boat.__________

Pascal's Principle (pages 432–436)

Transmitting Pressure in a Fluid (pages 433–434)

Key Concept: **When force is applied to a confined fluid, the change in pressure is transmitted equally to all parts of the fluid.**

- A fluid pushes against its container. This is called fluid pressure. When a container of fluid is squeezed, the fluid pressure increases.
- **Pascal's principle** says that when force is applied to a fluid in a closed container, pressure increases all through the fluid.
- You can see Pascal's principle with a water balloon. When you push in on one part of the balloon, other parts of the balloon bulge out.
- A hydraulic device contains fluid. Force is applied to one part of the device. The change in fluid pressure can be used to multiply the force.

Answer the following questions. Use your textbook and the ideas above.

1. Read each word in the box. In each sentence below, fill in the correct word or words.

fluid	Pascal's principle	pressure

   a. The particles in a ____________________ push against their container.

   b. According to ____________________, pressure increases all through a fluid when a force is applied.

Name ______________________ Date ______________ Class ___________

2. Read the words in the box. Use the words to fill in the concept map about Pascal's principle.

Pressure	Force	Fluid

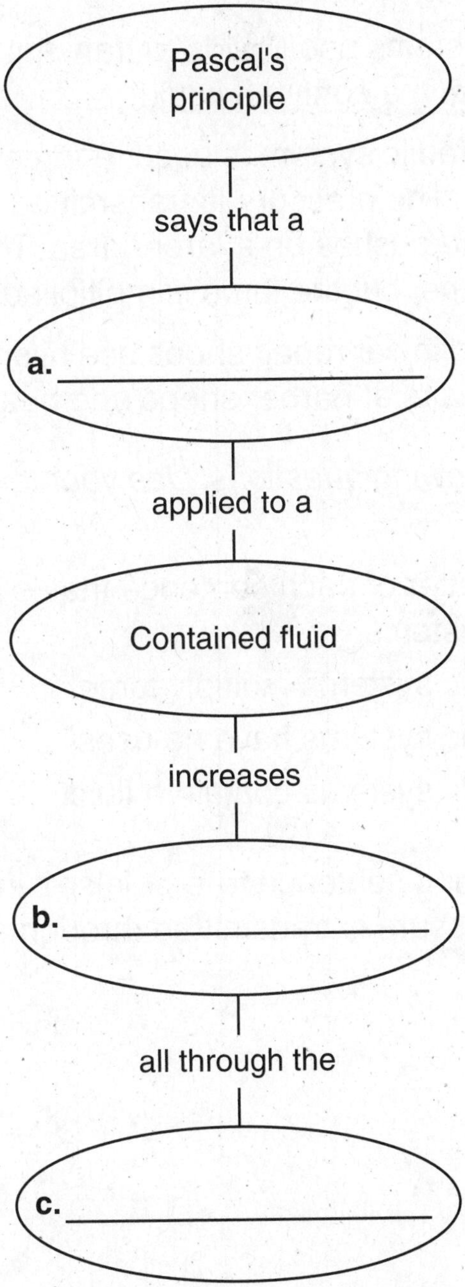

Pascal's principle

says that a

a. ______________________

applied to a

Contained fluid

increases

b. ______________________

all through the

c. ______________________

Hydraulic Systems (pages 435–436)

Key Concept: **A hydraulic system multiplies force by applying the force to a small surface area. The increase in pressure is then transmitted to another part of the confined fluid, which pushes on a larger surface area.**

- Hydraulic systems use liquids to transmit pressure and multiply force in a confined liquid.
- When a hydraulic system is used, a force is applied to a small area. The pressure is transmitted through the fluid. The fluid pushes on a larger area. The pressure stays the same, but the force is multiplied.
- The lifts used in car repair shops use hydraulic systems. So do the chairs at barber shops and beauty salons.

Answer the following questions. Use your textbook and the ideas above.

3. Circle the letter of each sentence that is true about hydraulic systems.

   a. Hydraulic systems multiply force.

   b. Hydraulic systems have no uses.

   c. Hydraulic systems contain a fluid.

4. Is the following sentence true or false? In a hydraulic system, pressure is transmitted through a fluid.

   ____

Bernoulli's Principle

(pages 437–441)

Pressure and Moving Fluids (page 438)

Key Concept: **Bernoulli's principle states that as the speed of a moving fluid increases, the pressure exerted by the fluid decreases.**

- **Bernoulli's principle** says that the faster a fluid moves, the less pressure it exerts.
- Fluid moves from places with high pressure to places with low pressure. When you suck on a drinking straw, you make an area of low pressure in the straw. This causes the fluid to move up the straw.

Answer the following questions. Use your textbook and the ideas above.

1. Is the following sentence true or false? The faster a fluid moves, the more pressure it exerts. __________

2. Circle the letter of what happens when a fluid moves faster.
   - **a.** It exerts more pressure.
   - **b.** The pressure it exerts does not change.
   - **c.** It exerts less pressure.

3. Fluids move from places with high pressure to places with ____________________ pressure.

Applying Bernoulli's Principle (pages 439–441)

Key Concept: **Bernoulli's principle helps explain how planes fly. It also helps explain how an atomizer works, why smoke rises up a chimney, and how a flying disk glides through the air.**

- Airplane wings are curved so air moves faster over the top. There is less pressure on top of the wing. Fluid pressure pushes the airplane wing upward.
- **Lift** is an upward force due to different air pressure above and below an object.
- Wind moves air over a chimney. The air pressure is lower at the top of the chimney than at the bottom. Smoke moves up the chimney because of the different air pressure.

Answer the following questions. Use your textbook and the ideas above.

4. What is lift?

a. an upward force

b. a downward force

c. a force that pushes to the side

5. Label the picture to show where air is moving faster and slower.

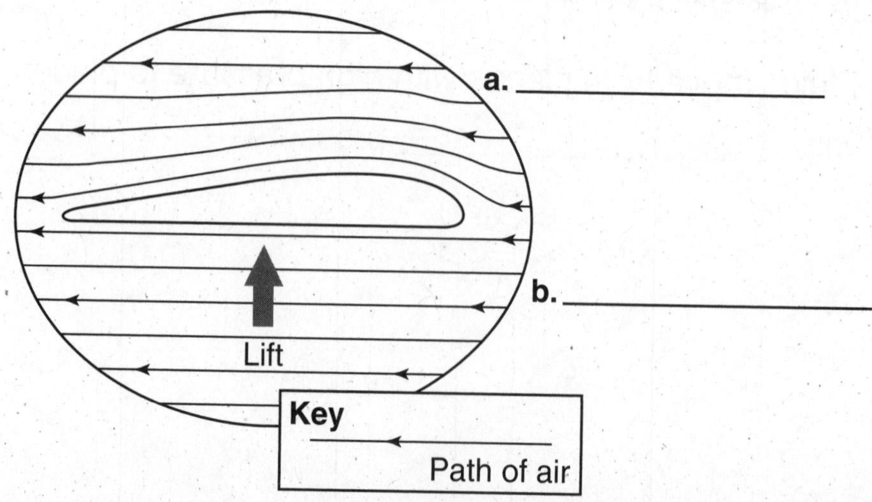

Earth in Space (pages 464–471)

How Earth Moves (pages 465–467)

Key Concept: **Earth moves through space in two major ways: rotation and revolution.**

- **Rotation** is spinning. Earth rotates on its axis. Earth's **axis** is an imaginary line that passes through Earth's center and the North and South poles.
- Earth's rotation causes day and night. As Earth rotates from west to east, the sun appears to move across the sky. The sun is not really moving. Earth's rotation makes it appear to move. It takes Earth about 24 hours to make one rotation.
- Earth also moves around the sun. This movement is called revolution. **Revolution** is the movement of one object around another.
- The path that Earth follows around the sun is called an **orbit**. Earth takes one year to travel all the way around the sun in its orbit.

Answer the following questions. Use your textbook and the ideas above.

1. The picture shows the planet Earth. Draw a line through the picture that shows Earth's axis.

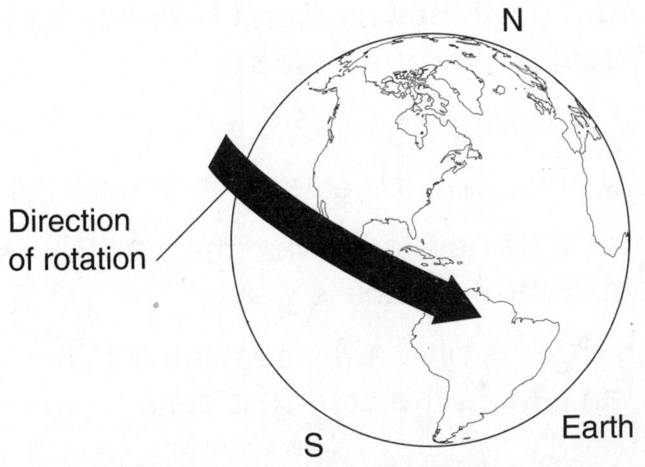

2. The picture shows Earth's revolution around the sun. Label Earth and the sun.

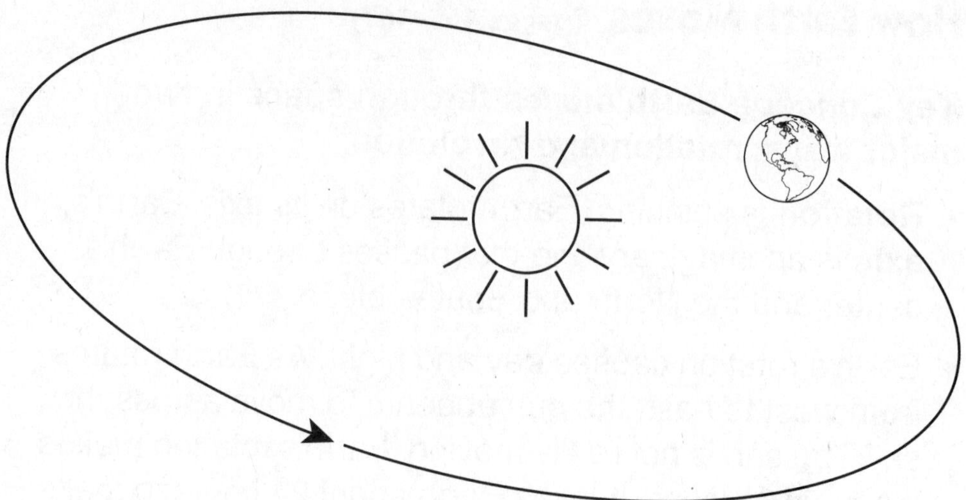

3. Draw a line from each term to its meaning.

Term	Meaning
axis	a. the movement of one object around another object
rotation	b. the imaginary line that passes through Earth's center and the North and South poles
revolution	c. the spinning of Earth

The Seasons on Earth (pages 468–471)

***Key Concept:* Earth has seasons because its axis is tilted as it revolves around the sun.**

- Earth's axis is tilted, or slanted.
- Earth is warmer near the equator than near the poles.
- In summer, Earth is tilted toward the sun. Day is longer than night. Earth's surface is warm.
- In winter, Earth is tilted away from the sun. Night is longer than day. Earth's surface is cold.

Answer the following questions. Use your textbook and the ideas on page 180.

4. Circle the letter of each sentence that is true about seasons on Earth.

a. In summer, Earth tilts toward the sun.

b. Earth's axis does not slant.

c. In winter, Earth's axis tilts away from the sun.

5. Read each word in the box. In each sentence below, fill in one of the words.

winter	spring	summer

a. The days are longer in ______________________.

b. The days are shorter in ______________________.

6. Fill in the blanks in the table below about Earth's tilt and the seasons.

Seasons in the Northern Hemisphere		
Season	**Length of Daytime**	**How the Northern Hemisphere Tilts**
Summer	longer than night	**b.** ______________
Winter	**a.** ______________	away from the sun

Gravity and Motion (pages 474–477)

Gravity (pages 474–475)

***Key Concept:* The strength of the force of gravity between two objects depends on two factors: the masses of the objects and the distance between them.**

- A **force** is a push or a pull.
- **Gravity** is the force that attracts all objects toward each other. Gravity works between objects that are not in contact. Gravity causes a book to fall if the book is dropped.
- **Mass** is the amount of matter in an object. The more mass an object has, the greater its force of gravity.
- Because of gravity, Earth pulls on the moon. The moon also pulls on Earth.
- The force of gravity is stronger when two objects are close together. The force of gravity gets weaker if the two objects are farther apart.

Answer the following questions. Use your textbook and the ideas above.

1. Read each word in the box. In each sentence below, fill in one of the words.

force	pull	gravity	mass

   a. The force that attracts all objects toward each other is called ____________________.

   b. The amount of matter in an object is called ____________________.

   c. A push or pull is called a ____________________.

2. Circle the letter of each sentence that is true about gravity.
   a. Gravity attracts objects toward each other.
   b. The more mass an object has, the greater its force of gravity is.
   c. The force of gravity is stronger when two objects are farther apart.

3. Is the following sentence true or false? Gravity is a force that pushes all objects away from each other.

   ____

Inertia and Orbital Motion (pages 476–477)

Key Concept: **Isaac Newton concluded that two factors—inertia and gravity—combine to keep Earth in orbit around the sun and the moon in orbit around Earth.**

- Objects that are moving tend to stay in motion. Objects that are not moving tend to stay still, or at rest. This tendency of an object to not change its motion is called **inertia**.
- Suppose you are in a car that stops suddenly. You will keep moving forward because of inertia.
- Isaac Newton stated his ideas about inertia as a scientific law. **Newton's first law of motion** says that an object at rest will stay at rest. The law also says that an object in motion will stay in motion.
- Earth's gravity keeps the moon from moving in a straight line. The moon's inertia keeps the moon moving ahead. The two forces combine to keep the moon revolving around Earth.

Answer the following questions. Use your textbook and the ideas on page 183.

4. Read each word in the box. In each sentence below, fill in one of the words.

inertia	motion	gravity

a. A moving object keeps moving because of

______________________.

b. The moon keeps moving ahead because of

______________________.

c. Earth's ______________________ keeps the moon from moving in a straight line.

5. Look at the picture below. Draw an arrow to show the direction of Earth's pull of gravity on the moon.

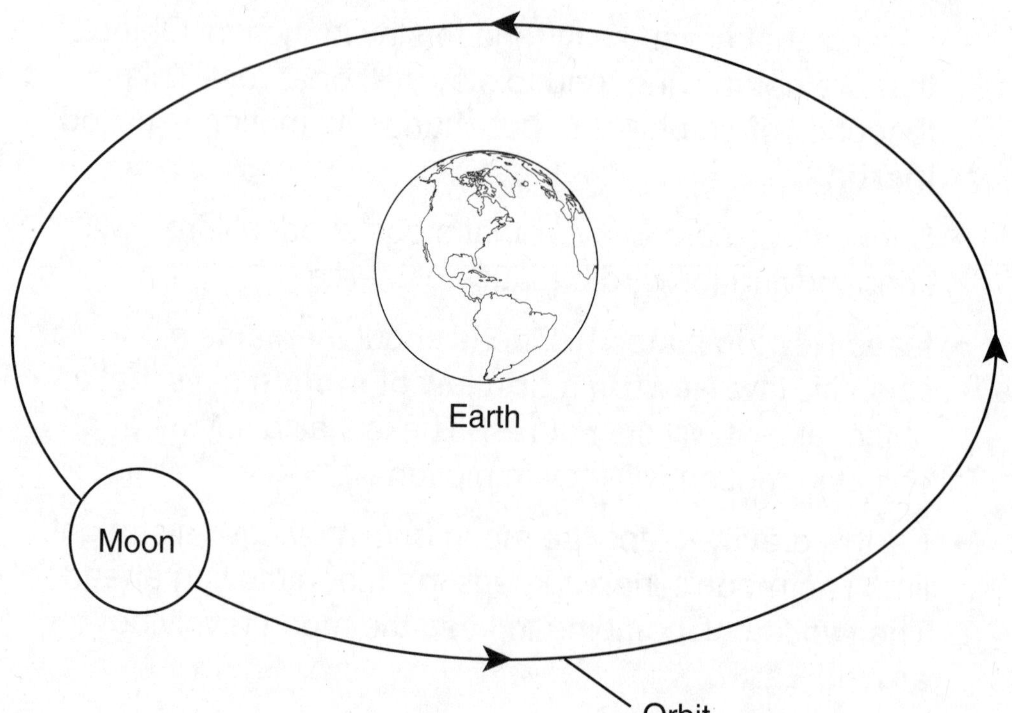

Phases, Eclipses, and Tides

(pages 478–485)

Motions of the Moon (page 478)

Key Concept: **The changing relative positions of the moon, Earth, and sun cause the phases of the moon, eclipses, and tides.**

- The moon rotates once on its axis in the same amount of time as it revolves around Earth.
- As the moon and Earth move, their positions change in relation to each other. Their positions also change in relation to the sun.

Answer the following question. Use your textbook and the ideas above.

1. Circle the letter of each sentence that is true about the moon.
   - **a.** The moon revolves around Earth.
   - **b.** The moon does not move.
   - **c.** The positions of Earth and the moon change.

Phases of the Moon (pages 479–481)

Key Concept: **The phase of the moon you see depends on how much of the sunlit side of the moon faces Earth.**

- The moon does not give off its own light. The moon reflects light from the sun.
- The moon appears to have different shapes at different times. These different shapes of the moon that you see are called **phases**.

- As the moon revolves around Earth, you see the moon from different angles. You cannot always see all of the part of the moon that is lit by the sun.

Answer the following questions. Use your textbook and the ideas on page 185 and above.

2. The different shapes of the moon that you see are called ________________.

3. Complete the table below to show what you see during the different phases of the moon.

Phases of the Moon	
Phase	**What You See**
New moon	The side of the moon facing Earth is dark.
First quarter	**a.** ________________
Full moon	**b.** ________________
Third quarter	**c.** ________________

Name ______________________ Date ________________ Class ____________

Eclipses (pages 481–483)

Key Concept: **When the moon's shadow hits Earth or Earth's shadow hits the moon, an eclipse occurs. A solar eclipse occurs when the moon passes directly between Earth and the sun, blocking sunlight from Earth.**

- An **eclipse** (ih KLIPS) is when an object in space comes between the sun and another object. For example, an eclipse occurs when the moon comes between the sun and Earth.
- Sometimes the moon moves between Earth and the sun. The moon blocks sunlight from reaching Earth. A **solar eclipse** occurs when a new moon blocks your view of the sun.

Answer the following questions. Use your textbook and the ideas above.

4. A(An) ______________________ is when an object in space comes between the sun and another object.

5. The drawing below shows the sun, the moon, and Earth during a solar eclipse. Draw lines from the moon to Earth that show the shadow.

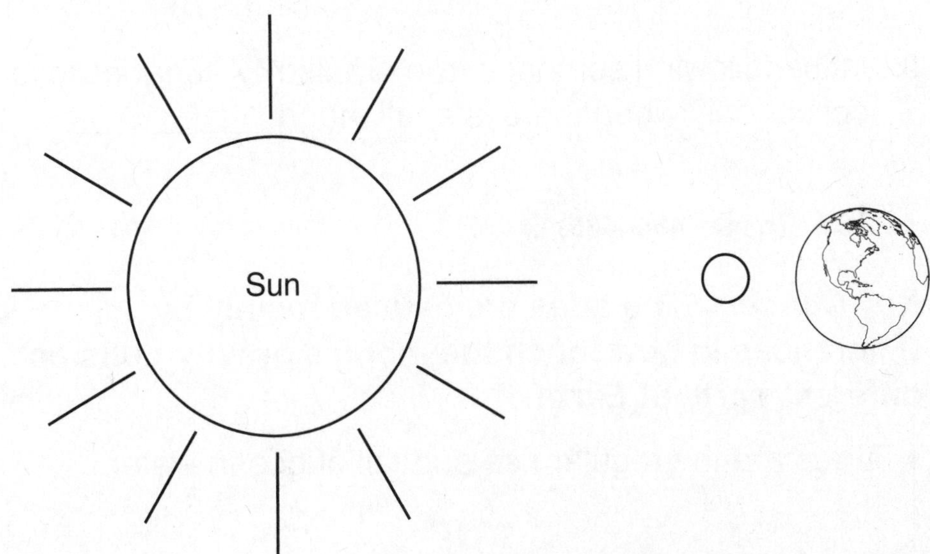

6. Is the following sentence true or false? A solar eclipse occurs when a full moon blocks your view of the sun.

   ____

Key Concept: **During a lunar eclipse, Earth blocks sunlight from reaching the moon.**

- A **lunar eclipse** occurs when Earth is between the moon and the sun.
- In a lunar eclipse, Earth's shadow hits the moon.
- A lunar eclipse occurs when there is a full moon.

Answer the following questions. Use your textbook and the ideas above.

7. Read each word in the box. In each sentence below, fill in the correct word or words.

solar eclipse	lunar eclipse	umbra

   a. Earth comes directly between the moon and the sun in a(an) ____________________.

   b. In a(an) ____________________, the moon's shadow hits Earth.

8. Is the following sentence true or false? A lunar eclipse occurs only when there is a full moon. __________

Tides (pages 484–485)

Key Concept: **The tides are caused mainly by differences in how much the moon's gravity pulls on different parts of Earth.**

- **Tides** are the regular rise and fall of ocean water.

- The moon's gravity causes tides. The force of the moon's gravity causes ocean water on Earth to move higher in some places and lower in other places.
- The sun's gravity also pulls on Earth's ocean waters.
- During a new moon, the sun, moon, and Earth are lined up in a straight line. The combined forces of the sun and the moon cause spring tides. A **spring tide** is the highest possible high tide.
- Sometimes, the sun, moon, and Earth form a right angle. This arrangement produces a neap tide. A **neap tide** is the lowest possible high tide.

Answer the following questions. Use your textbook and the ideas on page 188 and above.

9. Read the words in the box. In each sentence below, fill in the correct word or words.

tides	spring tide	neap tide

a. When the sun, moon, and Earth are lined up in a straight line, a ____________________ occurs.

b. The regular rise and fall of ocean water are ____________________.

c. When the sun, moon, and Earth form a right angle, a ____________________ occurs.

10. Circle the letter of each sentence that is true about tides.

a. The moon's gravity causes tides.

b. The sun's gravity also causes tides.

c. The sun's gravity and the moon's gravity do not combine.

Earth's Moon (pages 488–491)

The Moon's Surface (page 488)

***Key Concept:* Features on the moon's surface include maria, craters, and highlands.**

- A **telescope** makes faraway objects appear closer.
- The moon's surface has dark, flat areas called **maria** (MAH ree uh). Maria are flat areas of hardened rock.
- **Craters** are large, round pits on the moon. Craters were caused when meteoroids crashed into the moon. A **meteoroid** is a chunk of rock or dust from space.
- Highlands are mountains that cover most of the moon's surface.

Answer the following questions. Use your textbook and the ideas above.

1. A scientific instrument that makes faraway objects appear closer is a(an) ____________________.

2. Draw a line from each term to its meaning.

Term	Meaning
maria	**a.** large, round pits on the moon
	b. dark, flat areas on the moon
craters	
	c. chunks of rock or dust from space
highlands	**d.** mountains on the moon
meteoroids	

Characteristics of the Moon (page 490)

Key Concept: **The moon is dry and airless. Compared to Earth, the moon is small and has large variations in its surface temperature.**

- There is no air on the moon. The moon has no atmosphere.
- The moon is about one-fourth the diameter of Earth.
- Temperatures on the moon range from very hot to very cold.
- The moon has no liquid water.

Answer the following questions. Use your textbook and the ideas above.

3. Circle the letter of the size of the moon.

a. about twice the diameter of Earth

b. about half the diameter of Earth

c. about one-fourth the diameter of Earth

4. The moon can get very hot and very ________________.

The Origin of the Moon (page 491)

Key Concept: **Scientists theorize that a planet-sized object collided with Earth to form the moon.**

- Very long ago, big rocks were moving around in space.
- Scientists think that one of these big rocks may have crashed into Earth. Material from Earth broke off. The broken off portion of Earth became the moon.

Answer the following question. Use your textbook and the ideas above.

5. The moon may have formed when a big rock crashed into ______________________.

The Science of Rockets (pages 502–507)

A History of Rockets (page 503)

Key Concept: **Rocket technology originated in China hundreds of years ago and gradually spread to other parts of the world.**

- A **rocket** is a device that sends gas in one direction to move in the opposite direction. A rocket sends gas out the back, causing the rocket to move forward.
- The first rockets were made in China in the 1100s. These rockets were arrows that could be set on fire and then shot with bows.
- The first modern rockets were built in the early 1900s.

Answer the following questions. Use your textbook and the ideas above.

1. A device that sends gas in one direction to move in the opposite direction is called a(an)

______________________.

2. Circle the letter of where the first rockets were made.

a. the United States

b. China

c. Russia

3. Circle the letter of when modern rockets began to be built.

a. 1700s

b. 1800s

c. 1900s

How Do Rockets Work? (pages 504–505)

Key Concept: **A rocket moves forward when gases shooting out the back of the rocket push it in the opposite direction.**

- A rocket burns fuel to make hot gases. The gases shoot out the back of the rocket. The force of gases shooting out the back of a rocket is called the action force.
- The gases shooting out the back of a rocket send the rocket forward. This force that moves the rocket forward is called the reaction force. The reaction force that sends a rocket forward is called **thrust**.
- The greater the thrust, the greater the rocket's velocity. **Velocity** is speed in one direction.

Answer the following questions. Use your textbook and the ideas above.

4. Draw a line from each term to its meaning.

Term	Meaning
thrust	**a.** speed in one direction
velocity	**b.** the reaction force that sends a rocket forward

5. Circle the letter of the sentence that is true about thrust and the velocity of a rocket.

a. The less the thrust, the greater the velocity.

b. Thrust has nothing to do with velocity.

c. The greater the thrust, the greater the velocity.

6. The picture shows two forces that act on a rocket. Each force is represented by an arrow. Circle the arrow in the picture that represents the thrust of the rocket.

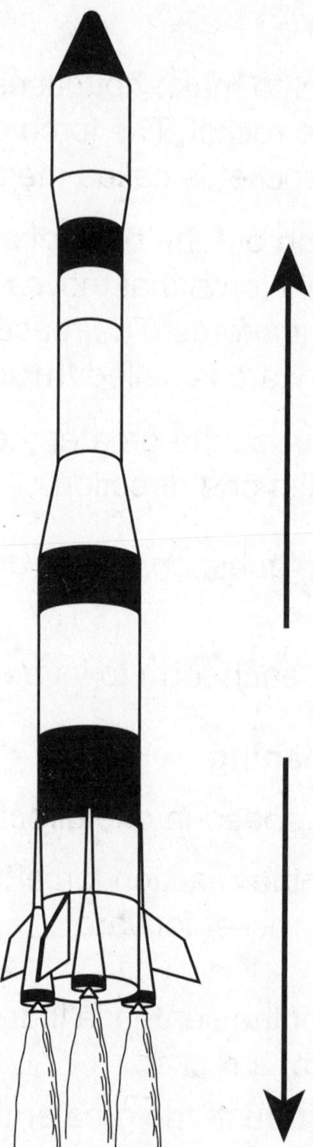

Multistage Rockets (pages 506–507)

***Key Concept:* The main advantage of a multistage rocket is that the total weight of the rocket is greatly reduced as the rocket rises.**

- A rocket made up of several small rockets is called a multistage rocket.
- In a multistage rocket, smaller rockets are placed one on top of another. Each of the smaller rockets is called a stage. The different stages fire one after the other.
- When a stage runs out of its fuel, the stage drops off and the next stage begins firing. The multistage rocket gets lighter and lighter as the stages drop off.
- At the end, there is just a single stage left, which is the very top of the rocket.

Answer the following questions. Use your textbook and the ideas above.

7. Circle the letter of each sentence that is true about multistage rockets.

a. The different stages all fire at once.

b. When a stage runs out of fuel, that stage drops off.

c. The different stages fire one after another.

8. Is the following sentence true or false? The total weight of a multistage rocket becomes lighter as the rocket rises. __________

The Space Program (pages 510–514)

The Race for Space (pages 510–511)

Key Concept: **The space race began in 1957 when the Soviets launched the satellite *Sputnik I* into orbit. The United States responded by speeding up its own space program.**

- The space race began in the 1950s. The space race was between the Soviet Union (now Russia) and the United States.
- A **satellite** is an object that revolves around another object in space. The moon is a natural satellite of Earth. A spacecraft orbiting Earth is an artificial satellite. "Artificial" means it is made by people.
- In 1957, the Soviet Union launched a satellite into space. The satellite was called *Sputnik I*. In 1958, the United States launched a satellite called *Explorer I*.
- The Soviet Union launched the first human into space in 1961. His name was Yuri Gagarin. The first American launched into space was Alan Shepard later in 1961. The first American to orbit Earth was John Glenn in 1962.

Answer the following questions. Use your textbook and the ideas above.

1. An object that revolves around another object in space is called a(an) ____________________.

2. Circle the letter of the correct answer. The space race was between the United States and

a. China.

b. the Soviet Union.

c. Germany.

3. The time line shows important events in the race for space. Read the events listed in the box. On the time line below, fill in the blanks.

Explorer I launched	John Glenn orbits Earth

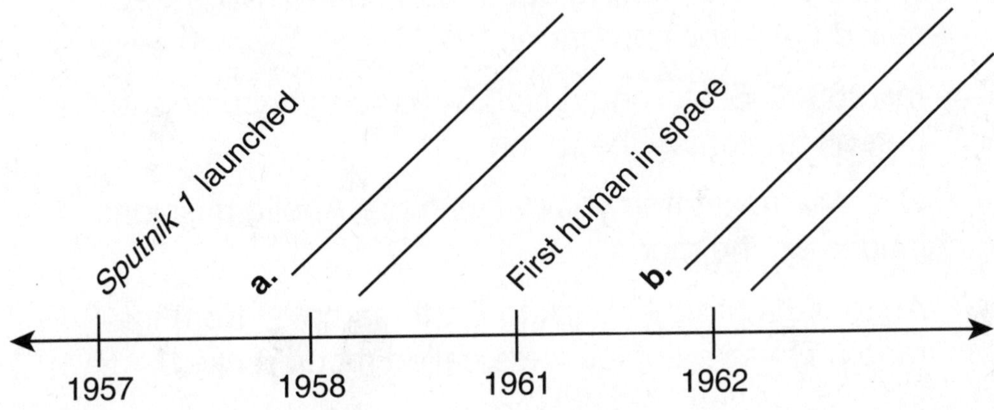

4. Circle the letter of the first human launched into space.

a. John Glenn

b. Alan Shepard

c. Yuri Gagarin

Missions to the Moon (pages 512–514)

Key Concept: **The American effort to land astronauts on the moon was named the Apollo program.**

- President John F. Kennedy set a goal in 1961. He said the United States would send a man to the moon within ten years. The effort to put a man on the moon was called the Apollo program.
- In 1969, U.S. astronaut Neil Armstrong became the first person to step on the moon.
- Over the next three years, five more Apollo missions landed on the moon.
- Astronauts brought back to Earth samples from the moon. These samples were called moon rocks.

Answer the following questions. Use your textbook and the ideas above.

5. Circle the letter of the first person to step on the moon.

a. Yuri Gagarin

b. Neil Armstrong

c. Buzz Aldrin

6. Circle the letter of the name of the U.S. program to put a man on the moon.

a. Lunar program

b. Moon program

c. Apollo program

7. Is the following sentence true or false? Astronauts brought rocks back to Earth from the moon.

____

Exploring Space Today (pages 515–519)

Working in Space (pages 516–517)

Key Concept: **NASA has used space shuttles to perform many important tasks. These include taking satellites into orbit, repairing damaged satellites, and carrying astronauts and equipment to and from space stations. A space station provides a place where long-term observations and experiments can be carried out in space.**

- A **space shuttle** is a spacecraft that can carry people into space. A space shuttle can then return to Earth and land like an airplane. A space shuttle can be used many times.
- A **space station** is a large satellite where people can live and work. The International Space Station is in orbit around Earth.

Answer the following questions. Use your textbook and the ideas above.

1. Read each word in the box. In each sentence below, fill in the correct words.

space station	space shuttle	space orbit

a. A large satellite where people can live is called a ____________________.

b. A spacecraft that can carry people into space is called a ____________________.

2. Circle the letter of each sentence that is true about space shuttles.

a. They cannot return to Earth.

b. They return to Earth like an airplane.

c. They can be used many times.

3. Circle the letter of the picture of the International Space Station.

a.

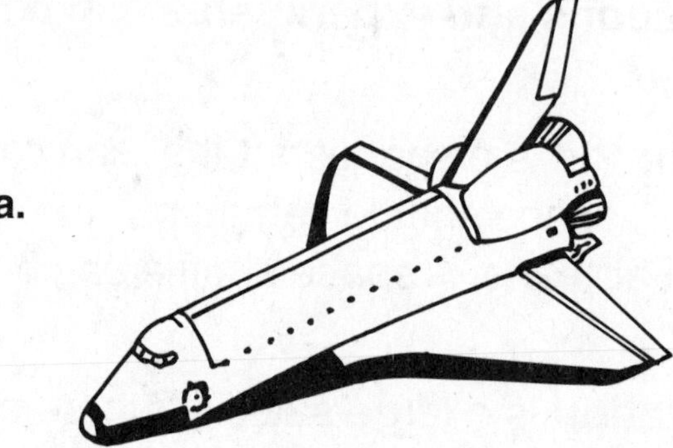

b.

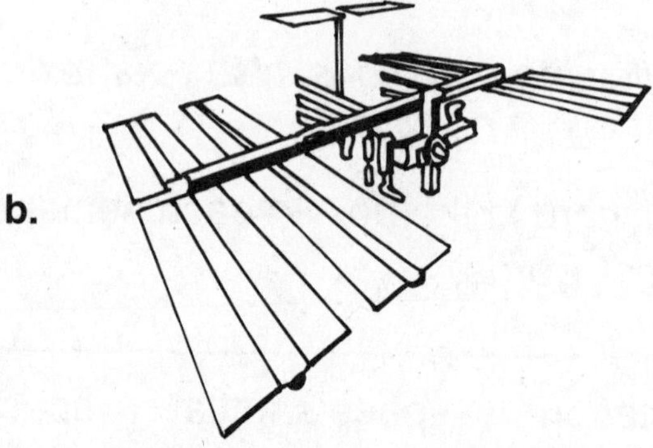

c.

Space Probes (pages 518–519)

Key Concept: **Each space probe has a power system to produce electricity, a communication system to send and receive signals, and scientific instruments to collect data and perform experiments.**

- A **space probe** is a spacecraft that carries scientific instruments into space. The instruments collect information. No humans are on board a space probe.
- Some space probes land on other planets. Some space probes fly around other planets.
- Some space probes have small robots called rovers. Rovers move around on the surface of a planet and collect information.
- Space probes have been sent to all planets except Pluto.

Answer the following questions. Use your textbook and the ideas above.

4. Draw a line from each term to its description.

Term	Description
space probe	**a.** a small robot that can move around on a planet
rover	**b.** a spacecraft that carries scientific instruments into space

5. Circle the letter of each sentence that is true about space probes.

a. Space probes have been sent to all nine planets.

b. Some space probes land on planets.

c. Some space probes fly around planets.

Using Space Science on Earth

(pages 520–524)

The Challenges of Space (page 521)

***Key Concept:* Conditions in space that differ from those on Earth include near vacuum, extreme temperatures, and microgravity.**

- A **vacuum** is a place that has no matter. Most of space is a vacuum. There is no air in space. Astronauts in space must carry oxygen to breathe.
- There is no air in space to hold the sun's heat. As a result, temperatures are usually very low in space.
- A feeling of having no weight is called **microgravity**. Astronauts in orbit feel microgravity.

Answer the following questions. Use your textbook and the ideas above.

1. Read each word in the box. In each sentence below, fill in one of the words.

microgravity	matter	condition

a. A vacuum is a place that has no

______________________.

b. A feeling of having no weight is called

______________________.

2. Circle the letter of the reason why astronauts must carry oxygen in space.

a. They feel microgravity in space.

b. There is no air in space.

c. They can feel no heat in space.

Space Spinoffs (pages 522–523)

Key Concept: **The space program has developed thousands of products that affect many aspects of modern society, including consumer products, new materials, medical devices, and communications satellites.**

- A **space spinoff** is something that was designed for space but is now used on Earth. Space spinoffs include things you can buy in stores. They also include new materials and medical devices.
- A joystick you use with computer games is an example of a space spinoff. So is the bar scanner you see in stores.
- Some new materials created for use in space are now used on Earth. An example is the material used for invisible dental braces.
- Some devices developed for space are used in medicine. For example, most hospitals use computer imaging developed for use on the moon.

Answer the following questions. Use your textbook and the ideas above.

3. A space spinoff is something that was designed for space but is now used on ____________________.

4. Circle the letter of each example of a space spinoff.
   a. game joystick
   b. invisible dental braces
   c. pacemakers

Satellites (page 524)

***Key Concept:* Satellites are used for communications and for collecting weather data and other scientific data.**

- Hundreds of satellites are in orbit around Earth. These satellites include observation satellites and communications satellites.
- The purpose of an observation satellite may be to track weather on Earth. Observation satellites collect data using remote sensing. **Remote sensing** is when information about Earth and other space objects is collected without direct contact.
- The purpose of a communications satellite is to relay signals from one part of Earth to another. These signals include television signals, radio signals, and telephone signals.

Answer the following questions. Use your textbook and the ideas above.

5. Is the following sentence true or false? There are only five satellites in orbit around Earth. __________

6. Collecting information about Earth without direct contact is an example of ____________________.

7. Complete the concept map about satellites.

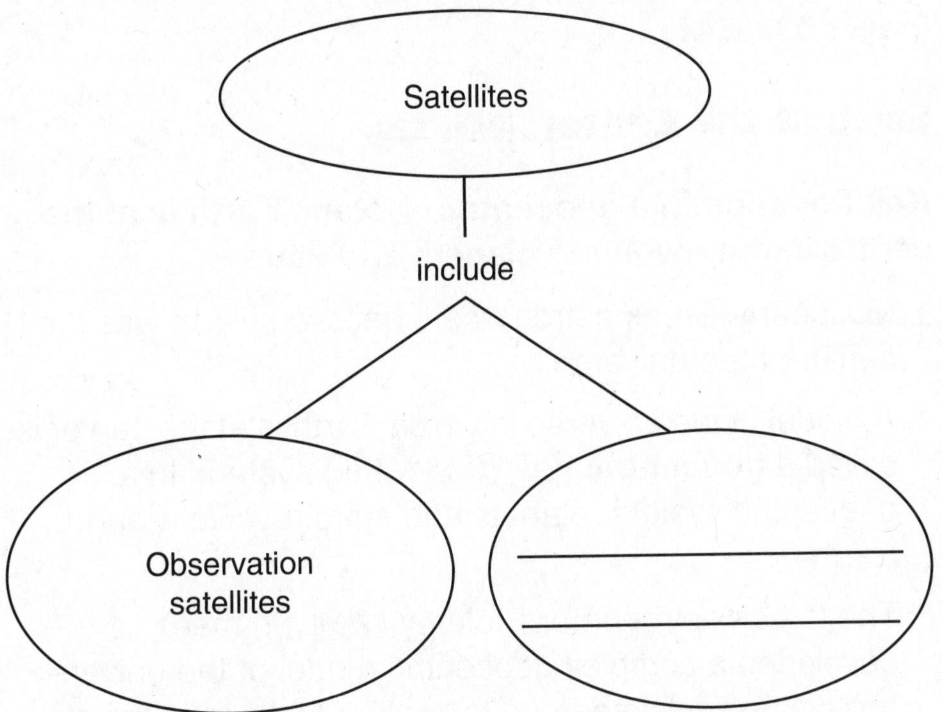

8. Circle the letter of the purpose of a communications satellite.

a. to track weather on Earth

b. to collect data from other planets

c. to relay signals from one part of Earth to another

Observing the Solar System

(pages 538–544)

Earth at the Center (page 539)

Key Concept: **In a geocentric system, Earth is at the center of the revolving planets and stars.**

- Most early Greek astronomers believed Earth was the center of the universe.
- A model of the universe in which Earth is at the center is called a **geocentric** (jee oh SEN trik) system. In a geocentric system, planets and stars revolve around Earth.
- The Greek astronomer Ptolemy (TAHL uh mee) developed a complex geocentric model of the universe. Ptolemy's model seemed to explain motions in the sky. Most people believed in Ptolemy's model until the 1500s.

Answer the following questions. Use your textbook and the ideas above.

1. In a geocentric system, planets and stars revolve around ______________________.

2. Circle the letter of the Greek astronomer who developed a geocentric model of the universe.
   a. Ptolemy
   b. Newton
   c. Copernicus

Sun at the Center (page 540)

Key Concept: **In a heliocentric system, Earth and the other planets revolve around the sun. Copernicus worked out the arrangement of the known planets and how they move around the sun. Galileo used the newly invented telescope to make discoveries that supported the heliocentric model.**

- A system in which the sun is at the center is called a **heliocentric** (hee lee oh SEN trik) system. Earth and other planets revolve around the sun in a heliocentric system.
- In 1543, a Polish astronomer named Nicolaus Copernicus developed a good heliocentric model of the universe.
- In the 1600s, the Italian scientist Galileo Galilei made discoveries that supported the heliocentric model.

Answer the following questions. Use your textbook and the ideas above.

3. Circle the letter of the astronomer who developed a heliocentric model in the 1500s.

a. Ptolemy

b. Galileo

c. Copernicus

4. Circle the letter of the picture of a heliocentric model of the solar system.

a.

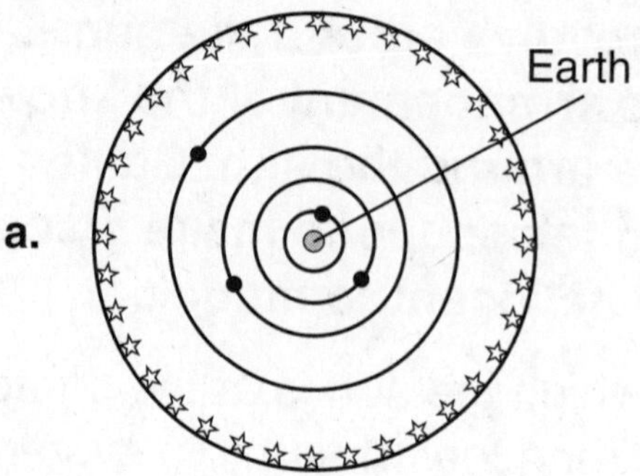

b.

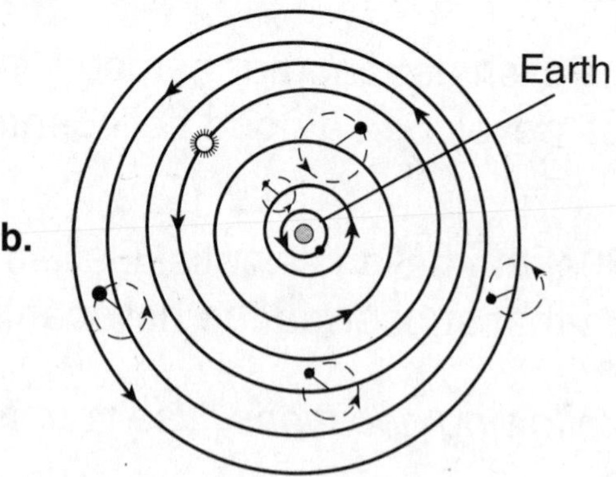

c.

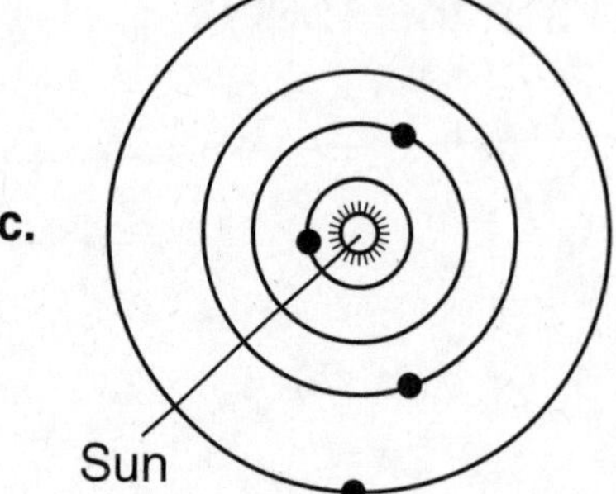

Motions of the Planets (pages 541–542)

Key Concept: **Kepler used Tycho Brache's data to develop three laws that describe the motions of the planets.**

- In the 1600s, the Danish astronomer Johannes Kepler discovered that the planets orbit the sun in a shape called an ellipse. An **ellipse** is an oval shape.

Answer the following question. Use your textbook and the idea above.

5. Circle the letter of the picture of an ellipse.

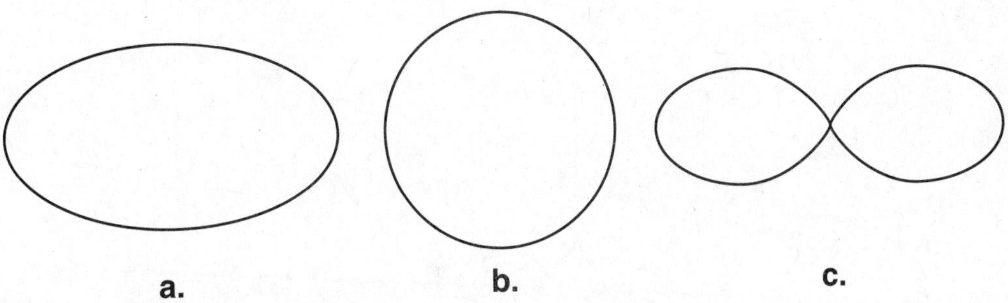

a. b. c.

Modern View of the Solar System (pages 543–544)

Key Concept: **Today we know that the solar system consists of the sun, the planets and their moons, and several kinds of smaller objects that revolve around the sun.**

- Early astronomers knew of only six planets—Mercury, Venus, Earth, Mars, Jupiter, and Saturn.
- Modern astronomers have discovered three more planets—Uranus, Neptune, and Pluto.
- Modern astronomers have identified many more objects in the solar system. These objects include **moons** around planets, comets, and asteroids.

Answer the following questions. Use your textbook and the ideas on page 209.

6. Circle the letter of each item that astronomers include in the solar system.

a. planets

b. the sun

c. the moons of the planets

7. Is the following sentence true or false? Early astronomers knew of all nine planets. __________

The Sun (pages 545–550)

Energy From the Sun (pages 546–547)

Key Concept: **The sun produces energy through nuclear fusion.**

- The sun does not have a solid surface. The sun is a ball of gas that glows. About three quarters of the sun's mass is hydrogen gas. About one quarter of the sun's mass is helium gas.
- The center of the sun is called the **core**. The sun produces energy at its core. The sun's energy comes from nuclear fusion. In **nuclear fusion**, hydrogen atoms join together to form helium.

Answer the following questions. Use your textbooks and the ideas above.

1. The sun is a ball of ______________________ that glows.

2. Circle the letter of the process that gives the sun its energy.

   a. glowing gas

   b. nuclear fusion

   c. streams of gas

The Sun's Interior (page 547)

Key Concept: **The sun's interior consists of the core, the radiation zone, and the convection zone.**

- The middle layer of the sun is called the **radiation zone**. Gas is tightly packed in the radiation zone.
- The outer layer of the sun is called the **convection zone**. Streams of gas move energy toward the sun's surface.

Answer the following question. Use your textbook and the ideas on page 211.

3. Read each word in the box. Use the words to fill in the blanks in the table about the sun's interior.

Radiation zone	Core	Convection zone
Atmosphere		

The Sun's Interior	
Layer of the Sun	**Location**
a. ______________________	the center
b. ______________________	the middle layer
c. ______________________	the outer layer

The Sun's Atmosphere (page 548)

Key Concept: **The sun's atmosphere includes the photosphere, the chromosphere, and the corona.**

- The inner layer of the sun's atmosphere is called the **photosphere** (FOH tuh sfeer). When you look at a picture of the sun, you see the photosphere.
- The middle layer of the sun's atmosphere is called the **chromosphere** (KROH muh sfeer).
- The outer layer of the sun's atmosphere is called the **corona**. The corona goes out into space for millions of kilometers.

- The corona gradually gets thinner. As the corona gets thinner, it becomes electrically charged particles. The electrically charged particles make up **solar wind**.

Answer the following questions. Use your textbook and the ideas on page 212 and above.

4. Draw a line from each term to its description.

Term	**Description**
corona	**a.** the inner layer of the sun's atmosphere
photosphere	**b.** the middle layer of the sun's atmosphere
chromosphere	**c.** the outer layer of the sun's atmosphere

5. Is the following sentence true or false? When you look at a picture of the sun, you see the corona. __________

6. As the sun's corona gets thinner, it becomes electrically charged particles. Circle the letter of what these electrically charged particles make up.

a. chromosphere

b. photosphere

c. solar wind

Features on the Sun (pages 548–550)

***Key Concept:* Features on or just above the sun's surface include sunspots, prominences, and solar flares.**

- There are dark spots called sunspots on the sun's surface. A **sunspot** is an area of gas that is cooler than the gases around that area.

- A **prominence** is a huge loop of gas that links different areas of sunspots.
- A **solar flare** is an explosion of gas from the sun's surface out into space.
- Solar flares can increase the amount of solar wind from the sun. Solar wind reaches Earth's atmosphere. Solar wind affects Earth's magnetic field.

Answer the following questions. Use your textbook and the ideas on page 213 and above.

7. Read each word in the box. In each sentence below, fill in the correct word or words.

prominence	sunspot	solar wind
solar flare		

a. An area of gas that is cooler than the gases around that area is a ______________________.

b. An explosion of gas from the sun's surface out into space is called a ______________________.

c. A huge loop of gas that links different areas of sunspots is a ______________________.

8. Solar flares can increase the amount of ______________________.

The Inner Planets (pages 552–559)

Introduction (page 552)

***Key Concept:* The four inner planets are small and dense and have rocky surfaces.**

- The four planets closest to the sun are called the inner planets. The four inner planets are Mercury, Venus, Earth, and Mars.
- The inner planets are called the **terrestrial planets**.
- The inner planets are more like one another than they are like the five outer planets. For example, the inner planets all have rocky surfaces.

Answer the following questions. Use your textbook and the ideas above.

1. The inner planets are called the

   ____________________ planets.

2. Circle the letter of how many inner planets there are.

   a. 2

   b. 4

   c. 6

Earth (pages 552–553)

***Key Concept:* Earth is unique in our solar system in having liquid water at its surface.**

- Earth has three main layers. The surface layer is the crust. Below the crust is the mantle. At Earth's center is the core.

- Most of Earth's surface—about 70 percent—is covered with water. Earth is the only planet with liquid water on its surface.
- Earth's gravity holds onto most gases. The gases around Earth make up Earth's atmosphere.

Answer the following questions. Use your textbook and the ideas on page 215 and above.

3. Is the following sentence true or false? Most of Earth's surface is covered with water. __________

4. Read each word in the box. Then fill in each blank in the picture below with one of the words.

mantle	crust	core

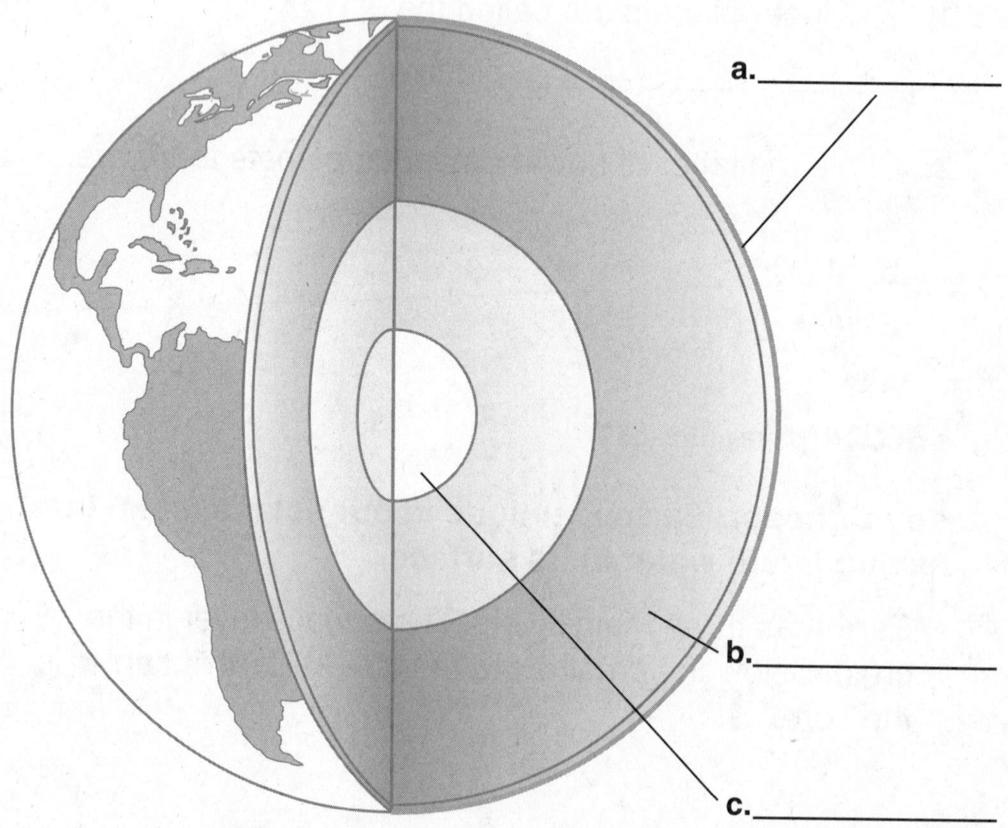

Name ______________________ Date ________________ Class ____________

Mercury (page 554)

***Key Concept:* Mercury is the smallest terrestrial planet and the planet closest to the sun.**

- Mercury is the closest planet to the sun. Mercury is the smallest of the inner planets. It is not much larger than Earth's moon.
- Mercury has almost no atmosphere because it has very weak gravity.
- Mercury has extreme temperatures on its surface. It is very hot during the day and very cold at night.

Answer the following questions. Use your textbook and the ideas above.

5. Circle the letter of each sentence that is true about Mercury.

a. It is the closest planet to the sun.

b. It has a very thick atmosphere.

c. It is the smallest of the inner planets.

6. The picture shows the sun and the inner planets. Circle the planet Mercury.

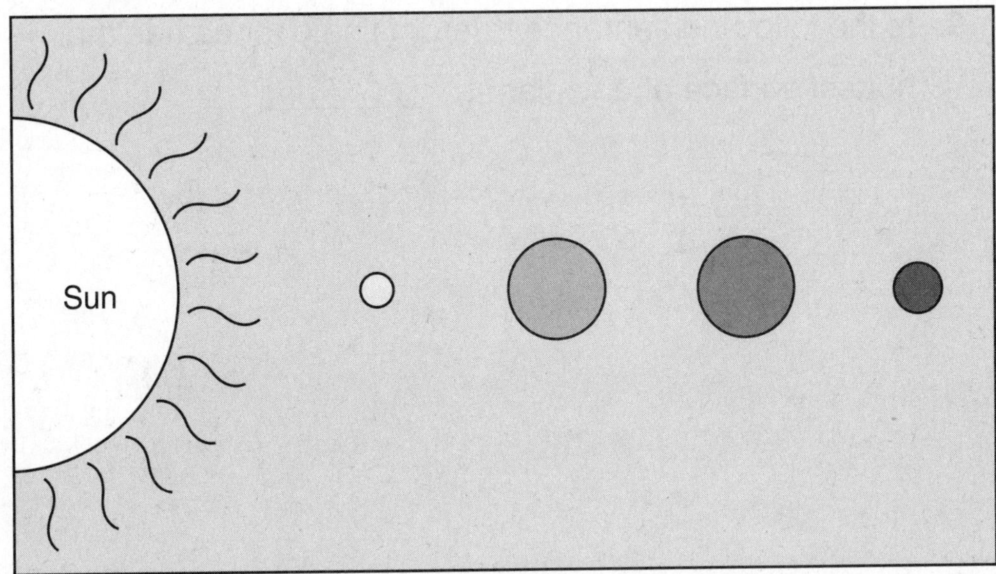

Venus (pages 555–556)

Key Concept: **Venus's density and internal structure are similar to Earth's. But, in other ways, Venus and Earth are very different.**

- Venus is very much like Earth in size and mass.
- Venus's atmosphere is very thick. It is always cloudy on Venus.
- Venus has the hottest surface of any planet. Venus's atmosphere traps the sun's heat. The trapping of heat by the atmosphere is called the **greenhouse effect**.

Answer the following questions. Use your textbook and the ideas above.

7. Circle the letter of each sentence that is true about Venus.

- **a.** It is much larger than Earth.
- **b.** It has a very thick atmosphere.
- **c.** It has no clouds in its atmosphere.

8. The trapping of ____________________ by Venus's atmosphere is called the greenhouse effect.

9. Is the following sentence true or false? Venus has the hottest surface of any planet. __________

Mars (pages 557–559)

***Key Concept:* Scientists think that a large amount of liquid water flowed on Mars's surface in the distant past.**

- Mars is called the "red planet" because it looks red from Earth.
- The surface of Mars has huge canyons and ancient coastlines. Scientists think that liquid water may have formed these features. There is no liquid water on Mars's surface now.
- Mars has two very small moons. They are called Phobos and Deimos.
- Many space probes have been sent to Mars.

Answer the following questions. Use your textbook and the ideas above.

10. Circle the letter of each sentence that is true about Mars.

  a. Mars is called the "red planet."

  b. There are two moons that orbit Mars.

  c. The surface of Mars is covered with water.

11. Is the following sentence true or false? No space probe has been sent to Mars. __________

12. What do scientists think formed the features on the surface of Mars? Circle the letter of the correct answer.

  a. the sun

  b. space probes

  c. water

The Outer Planets (pages 562–569)

Gas Giants and Pluto (page 563)

Key Concept: **The first four outer planets—Jupiter, Saturn, Uranus, and Neptune—are much larger and more massive than Earth, and they do not have solid surfaces.**

- The outer planets include Jupiter, Saturn, Uranus, Neptune, and Pluto.
- The first four outer planets—Jupiter, Saturn, Uranus, and Neptune—are called the **gas giants**. They are very large, and they do not have solid surfaces.
- The gas giants are made up mainly of hydrogen and helium.
- All the gas giants have many moons. Each gas giant is also surrounded by rings. A **ring** is a thin circle of small ice and rock particles around a planet.

Answer the following questions. Use your textbook and the ideas above.

1. Circle the letter of the sentence that is true about gas giants.

a. They have rocky surfaces.

b. They have no moons.

c. They do not have solid surfaces.

2. Each of the gas giants is surrounded by circles called

______________________.

3. Complete the concept map about the outer planets.

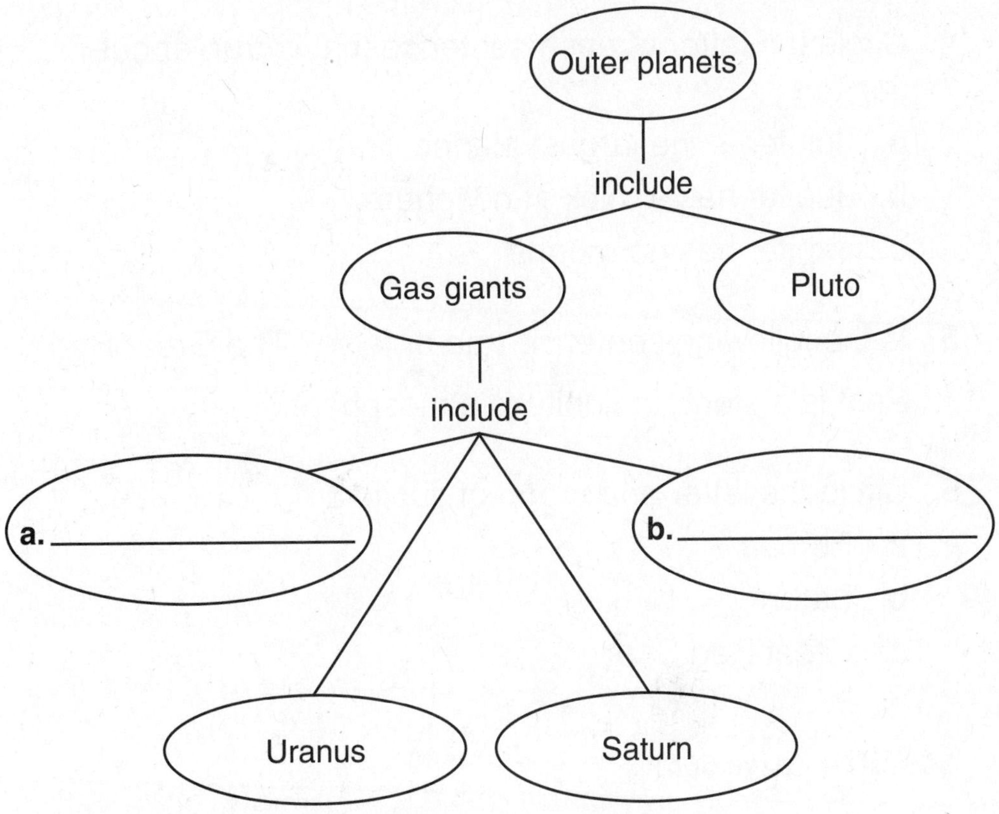

Jupiter (pages 564–565)

Key Concept: **Jupiter is the largest and most massive planet.**

- Jupiter's mass is about 2 1/2 times the mass of all the other planets combined.
- Jupiter has a thick atmosphere made up mainly of hydrogen and helium. A storm in Jupiter's atmosphere is called the Great Red Spot.
- Jupiter has more than 60 moons. The four largest moons are Io (EYE oh), Europa, Ganymede, and Callisto.

Answer the following questions. Use your textbook and the ideas on page 221.

4. Circle the letter of each sentence that is true about Jupiter.

a. Jupiter is the largest planet.

b. Jupiter has a thick atmosphere.

c. Jupiter has no moons.

5. Is the following sentence true or false? The Great Red Spot is a storm in Jupiter's atmosphere. __________

6. Circle the letter of a moon of Jupiter.

a. Europa

b. Saturn

c. Great Red Spot

Saturn (page 566)

***Key Concept:* Saturn has the most spectacular rings of any planet.**

- Saturn is the second-largest planet. Saturn's atmosphere is made up mostly of hydrogen and helium.
- Saturn has many rings. Saturn's rings are broad and thin.
- Saturn has more than 31 moons. Saturn's largest moon is named Titan. Titan is larger than the planet Mercury.

Answer the following questions. Use your textbook and the ideas above.

7. Is the following sentence true or false? Saturn is the second-largest planet. __________

8. The picture shows the sun and the planets of the solar system. Draw a circle around the planet Saturn.

9. Circle the letter of each sentence that is true about Saturn.

a. Saturn's rings are broad and thin.

b. Saturn's largest moon is named Titan.

c. Saturn's atmosphere is made up mostly of hydrogen and helium.

Uranus (page 567)

***Key Concept:* Uranus's axis of rotation is tilted at an angle of about 90 degrees from the vertical.**

- Uranus looks blue-green from Earth because there is methane gas in its atmosphere.
- Uranus is surrounded by a group of thin, flat rings.
- Uranus's axis is different than the axes of other planets. Uranus looks like it is rotating from top to bottom. Other planets look like they are rotating from side to side.
- Uranus has at least 27 moons. Uranus's five largest moons have icy surfaces with many craters.

Answer the following questions. Use your textbook and the ideas on page 223.

10. Circle the letter of each sentence that is true about Uranus.

- **a.** Uranus has no rings.
- **b.** Uranus has no moons.
- **c.** Uranus looks blue-green from Earth.

11. Is the following sentence true or false? Uranus looks like it is rotating from top to bottom. __________

Neptune (page 568)

Key Concept: **Neptune is a cold, blue planet. Its atmosphere contains visible clouds.**

- Neptune is much like Uranus in size and color. Neptune looks blue from Earth. Neptune's atmosphere has clouds.
- Scientists think that Neptune is shrinking.
- Neptune has at least 13 moons. Neptune's largest moon is called Triton.

Answer the following questions. Use your textbook and the ideas above.

12. Is the following sentence true or false? There are no clouds in Neptune's atmosphere. __________

13. Circle the letter of each sentence that is true about Neptune.

- **a.** Neptune's largest moon is called Triton.
- **b.** Scientists think that Neptune is shrinking.
- **c.** Neptune is much larger than Uranus.

Pluto (page 569)

Key Concept: **Pluto has a solid surface and is much smaller and denser than the other outer planets.**

- Pluto is the farthest planet from the sun. Pluto is very different than the gas giants. For example, Pluto has a solid surface.
- Pluto is smaller than Earth's moon. Pluto is so small that some astronomers do not think it should be called a planet.

Answer the following questions. Use your textbook and the ideas above.

14. Is the following sentence true or false? Pluto is the nearest planet to the sun. __________

15. Pluto is smaller than Earth's ____________________.

Comets, Asteroids, and Meteors (pages 572–575)

Comets (page 573)

***Key Concept:* Comets are loose collections of ice, dust, and small rocky particles whose orbits are usually very long, narrow ellipses.**

- A **comet** orbits the sun. A comet is made up of ice, dust, and small rocky particles. You can think of a comet as a "dirty snowball."
- The orbit of a comet is usually an ellipse that is very long and narrow.
- The brightest part of a comet is the head. A comet's head is made up of a **nucleus** and a **coma**. The nucleus is the solid core of a comet. The coma is a fuzzy outer layer made up of clouds of gas and dust.

Answer the following questions. Use your textbook and the ideas above.

1. Read each word in the box. In each sentence below, fill in one of the words.

coma	comet	nucleus	tail

   a. A "dirty snowball" that orbits the sun is a ____________________.

   b. The solid core of a comet is the ____________________.

   c. The fuzzy outer layer of a comet is the ____________________.

2. Is the following sentence true or false? A comet's orbit is usually a very long and narrow ellipse. __________

Asteroids (page 574)

***Key Concept:* Most asteroids revolve around the sun in fairly circular orbits between the orbits of Mars and Jupiter.**

- An **asteroid** is a rocky object that orbits the sun. Asteroids are too small to be planets.
- Most asteroids are in orbit between Mars and Jupiter. This region of the solar system is called the **asteroid belt**.
- Most asteroids are less than 1 kilometer in diameter. Some are much larger.
- Scientists think that asteroids are leftover pieces of rock from the early solar system.

Answer the following questions. Use your textbook and the ideas above.

3. A rocky object that orbits the sun and is too small to be a planet is a(an) ____________________.

4. Circle the letter of the location of the asteroid belt in the solar system.
   a. between Earth and Venus
   b. between Jupiter and Saturn
   c. between Mars and Jupiter

5. Is the following sentence true or false? Scientists think that asteroids are leftover pieces of rock from the early solar system. __________

Meteors (page 575)

***Key Concept:* Meteoroids come from comets or asteroids.**

- A **meteoroid** is a chunk of rock or dust in space.
- Some meteoroids form when asteroids crash into each other. Other meteoroids form when comets break apart.
- Meteoroids can enter Earth's atmosphere. When one does, friction between the meteoroid and the air produces a streak of light in the sky. A **meteor** is a streak of light in the night sky produced by a meteoroid.
- Most meteoroids burn up completely in Earth's atmosphere. However, some hit Earth's surface. Meteoroids that hit Earth's surface are called **meteorites**.

Answer the following questions. Use your textbook and the ideas above.

6. Circle the letter of each object that a meteoroid can come from.

a. Earth
b. comet
c. asteroid

7. Is the following sentence true or false? Meteoroids never enter Earth's atmosphere. __________

8. Read each word in the box. In each blank in the table below, fill in one of the words.

Meteor	Meteoroid	Meteorite

Rocks From Space	
Term	**Description**
a. ________________	a streak of light in the night sky
b. ________________	a meteoroid that hits Earth's surface
c. ________________	a chunk of rock or dust in space

Is There Life Beyond Earth? (pages 576–579)

Life on Earth (page 577)

Key Concept: **Earth has liquid water and a suitable temperature range and atmosphere for living things to survive.**

- All life that is not Earth life is called **extraterrestrial life**. No one knows if there are living things beyond Earth.
- Scientists talk about "life as we know it." Life as we know it lives on Earth, where there is liquid water, good temperatures, and an atmosphere. These conditions are sometimes called "Goldilocks conditions."
- "Goldilocks conditions" may or may not be necessary for life. No one knows for sure.

Answer the following questions. Use your textbook and the ideas above.

1. All life that is not Earth life is called

   ______________________ life.

2. Circle the letter of each condition that is included in "Goldilocks conditions."
   - **a.** good temperatures
   - **b.** an atmosphere
   - **c.** liquid water

3. Is the following sentence true or false? No one knows if there are living things beyond Earth. __________

Life Elsewhere in the Solar System?

(pages 578–579)

Key Concept: **Since life as we know it requires water, scientists hypothesize that Mars may have once had the conditions needed for life to exist.**

- Mars is the planet that is most like Earth. Scientists have looked for living things on Mars.
- The surface of Mars looks like it once had water.

Answer the following question. Use your textbook and the ideas above.

4. Circle the letter of why scientists think that life might exist on Mars.

a. The surface of Mars looks like it once had water.

b. There is evidence that Mars has the "Goldilocks conditions."

c. There is evidence that life on Mars came from Europa.

Key Concept: **If there is liquid water on Europa, there might also be life.**

- Europa is a moon of Jupiter. Many scientists think there could be life on Europa.

Answer the following question. Use your textbook and the ideas above.

5. Circle the letter of the planet Europa revolves around.

a. Mars

b. Saturn

c. Jupiter

Telescopes (pages 590–596)

Electromagnetic Radiation (page 591)

Key Concept: **The electromagnetic spectrum includes the entire range of radio waves, infrared radiation, visible light, ultraviolet radiation, X-rays, and gamma rays.**

- Energy that travels through space in the form of waves is called **electromagnetic** (ih lek troh mag NET ik) **radiation**.
- Light that you can see is called **visible light**. Visible light is one kind of electromagnetic radiation. There are many other kinds of electromagnetic radiation.
- Visible light has very short wavelengths. A **wavelength** is the distance between the top of one wave and the top of the next wave.
- The range of different wavelengths of electromagnetic waves is called a spectrum. The **spectrum** of all electromagnetic waves is called the electromagnetic spectrum.

Answer the following questions. Use your textbook and the ideas above.

1. Draw a line from each term to its meaning.

Term	**Meaning**
electromagnetic radiation	**a.** the light you can see
visible light	**b.** the range of different wavelengths
spectrum	**c.** energy that travels through space in the form of waves

2. The picture below shows a wave of electromagnetic radiation. Draw a line over the wave to show one wavelength.

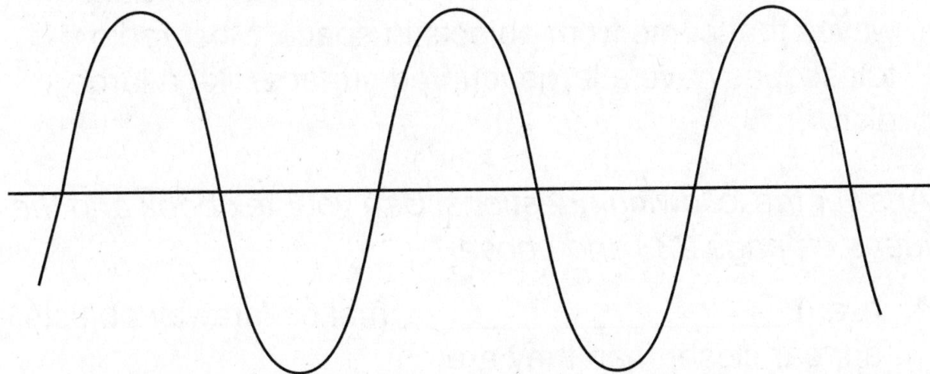

3. Circle the letter of each sentence that is true about electromagnetic radiation.

a. There are many types of electromagnetic radiation.

b. Visible light has very short wavelengths.

c. Energy cannot travel through space.

Types of Telescopes (pages 592–593)

Key Concept: **Telescopes are instruments that collect and focus light and other forms of electromagnetic radiation.**

- A telescope makes faraway objects appear closer than they are.
- A telescope that collects and focuses visible light is called an **optical telescope**. The two major types of optical telescopes are refracting telescopes and reflecting telescopes.
- A **refracting telescope** uses lenses to gather and focus light.

- A **reflecting telescope** uses a curved mirror to collect and focus light. The largest telescopes are reflecting telescopes.
- A **radio telescope** is a device used to collect radio waves that come from objects in space. Most radio telescopes have a large, curved surface, like a large dish.

Answer the following questions. Use your textbook and the ideas on page 233 and above.

4. A(an) ______________________ makes faraway objects appear closer than they are.

5. Complete the concept map about telescopes.

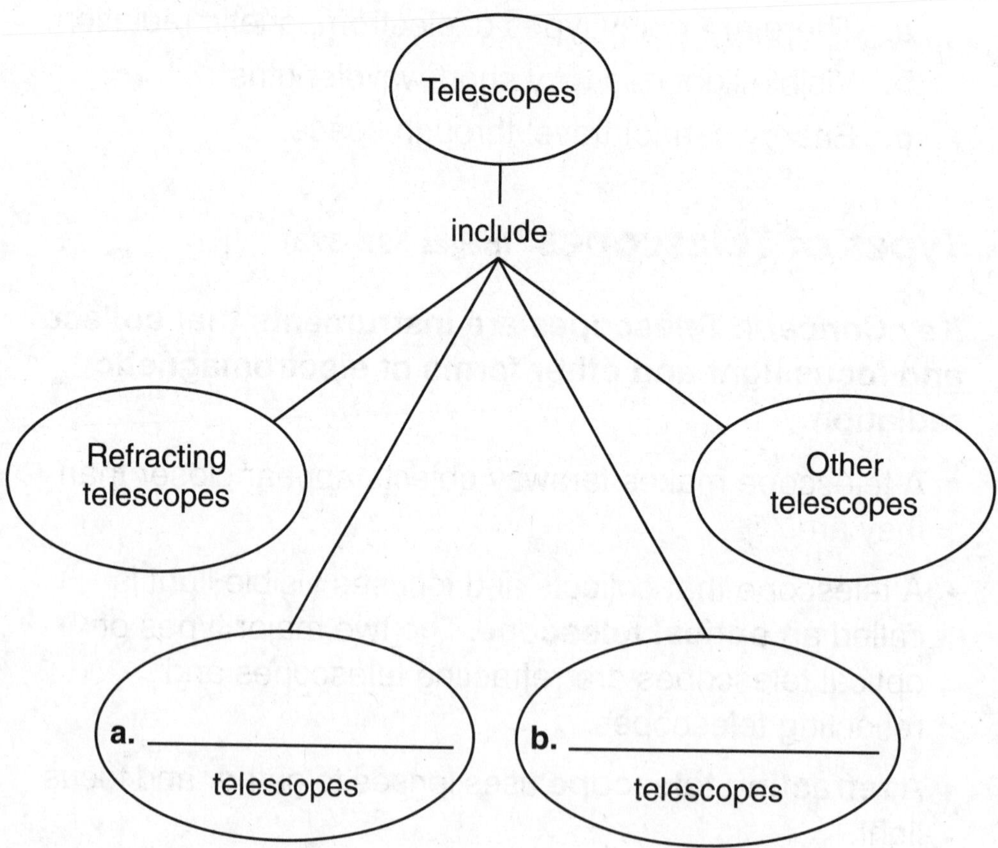

Observatories (pages 594–596)

Key Concept: **Many large observatories are located on mountaintops or in space.**

- An **observatory** is usually a building that has one or more telescopes. Some observatories are not in buildings, because they are located in space.
- Many observatories are on the tops of mountains because the sky is clearer on mountaintops. There are also no city lights on mountaintops. For example, one of the best observatories is on top of Mauna Kea, an old volcano on the island of Hawaii.
- The Hubble Space Telescope is a reflecting telescope in space high above Earth.

Answer the following questions. Use your textbook and the ideas above.

6. A building that has one or more telescopes is called a(an) ____________________.

7. Circle the letter of each sentence that is true about observatories.

a. Many observatories are on the tops of mountains.

b. One of the best observatories is on the island of Hawaii.

c. There are no observatories in space.

8. Is the following sentence true or false? The Hubble Space Telescope is a refracting telescope. __________

Characteristics of Stars

(pages 598–605)

Classifying Stars (pages 599–600)

Key Concept: **Characteristics used to classify stars include color, temperature, size, composition, and brightness.**

- A star's color gives clues about the star's temperature. The coolest stars appear red. The hottest stars appear blue.
- Very large stars are called giant stars or supergiant stars. Our sun is a medium-sized star. Most stars are smaller than the sun.
- Stars differ in their chemical make-ups. Astronomers use spectrographs to find out what elements are in a star. A **spectrograph** (SPEK truh graf) is a device that breaks light into colors. Scientists compare a star's light with the light produced by different elements to find out what elements are in the star.

Answer the following questions. Use your textbook and the ideas above.

1. Is the following sentence true or false? A star's color gives clues about the star's temperature. __________

2. Circle the letter of a device that breaks light into colors.
   a. spectrograph
   b. telescope
   c. observatory

3. Complete the concept map about characteristics used to classify stars.

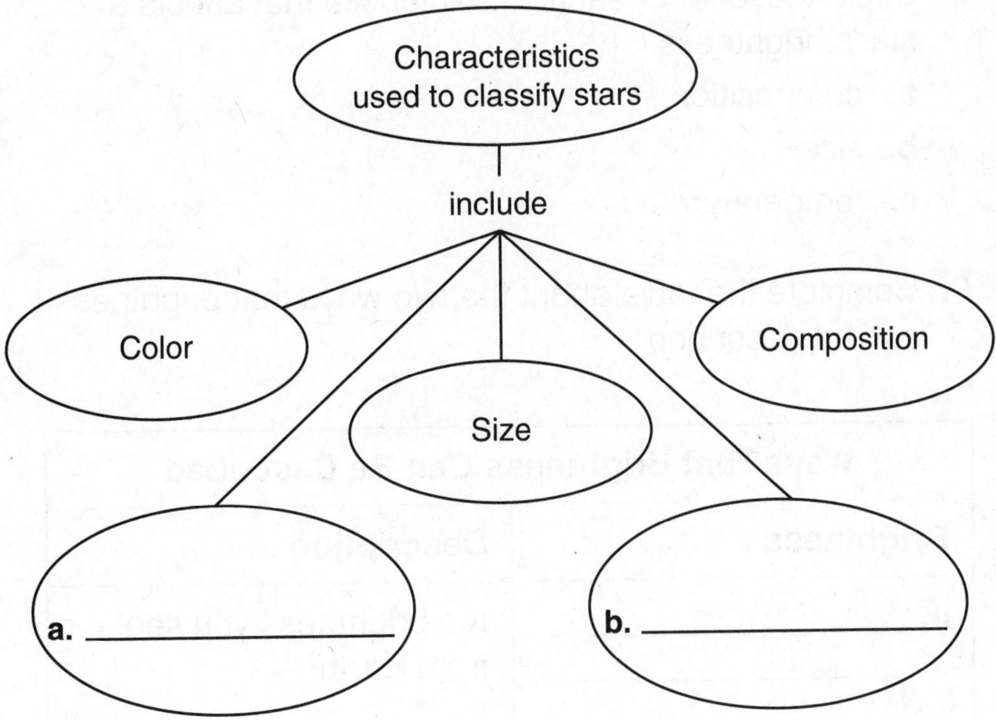

Brightness of Stars (pages 600–601)

***Key Concept:* The brightness of a star depends upon both its size and temperature.**

- Stars differ in how bright they are. How bright a star looks depends on its distance from Earth and how bright the star really is.
- A star's **apparent brightness** is the brightness you see from Earth. A hot, large star that is very far from Earth does not look very bright. But the sun looks very bright because it is so close to Earth.
- A star's **absolute brightness** is the brightness the star would have if all stars were the same distance from Earth.

Answer the following questions. Use your textbook and the ideas on page 237.

4. Circle the letter of each characteristic that affects a star's brightness.

a. composition

b. size

c. temperature

5. Complete the table about the two ways that brightness can be described.

Ways That Brightness Can Be Described	
Brightness	**Description**
a. ____________________	the brightness you see from Earth
b. ____________________	the brightness a star would have if all stars were the same distance from Earth

Measuring Distances to Stars (pages 602–603)

Key Concept: **Astronomers use a unit called the light-year to measure distances between the stars.**

- A **light-year** is the distance that light travels in one year. That distance is about 9.5 million million kilometers.
- A light-year is a unit of distance, not time. You could also measure distance on Earth in terms of time.

Answer the following questions. Use your textbook and the ideas on page 238.

6. The distance that light travels in one year is a(an) ______________________________.

7. Is the following sentence true or false? A light-year is a unit of distance, not time. ____________

***Key Concept:* Astronomers often use parallax to measure distances to nearby stars.**

- **Parallax** is the change in an object's position you seem to see when you change your own position. The object does not really change position. It only seems to change because you change your position.
- Astronomers use parallax. They measure how far a star seems to move when Earth moves from one side of the sun to the other. The distance the star seems to move tells an astronomer how far the star is from Earth.

Answer the following questions. Use your textbook and the ideas above.

8. The change in an object's position you seem to see when you change your own position is ______________________________.

9. Circle the letter of what astronomers use parallax for.

a. to measure distances to nearby stars

b. to compare the brightness of stars

c. to determine the elements found in stars

The Hertzsprung-Russell Diagram

(pages 604–605)

***Key Concept:* Astronomers use H-R diagrams to classify stars and to understand how stars change over time.**

- The **Hertzsprung-Russell diagram**, or the H-R diagram, shows how the surface temperature of stars is related to their absolute brightness.
- The points on the H-R diagram form a pattern. Most stars on the H-R diagram fall into a band that spreads from the top left corner to the bottom right corner. This band is called the main sequence. Stars in the main sequence are called **main-sequence** stars. About 90 percent of all stars are main-sequence stars.

Answer the following questions. Use your textbook and the ideas above.

10. The Hertzsprung-Russell diagram shows how the surface temperature of stars is related to absolute

______________________.

11. Most stars are ______________________ stars.

12. The picture shows a H-R diagram. The dots represent stars. Draw a line on the diagram to show about where the main sequence is.

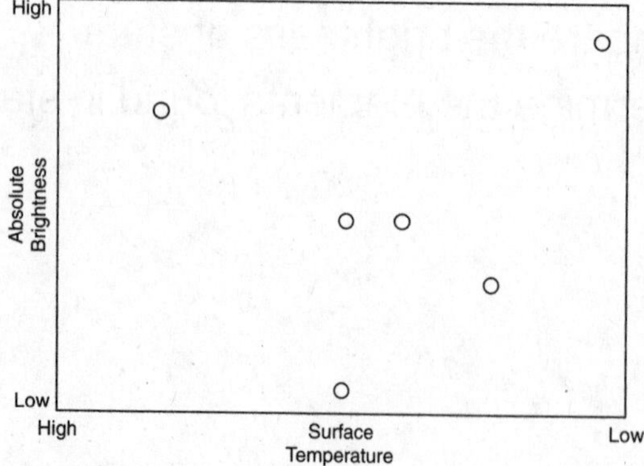

Lives of Stars (pages 608–613)

The Lives of Stars (page 609)

Key Concept: **A star is born when the contracting gas and dust from a nebula become so dense and hot that nuclear fusion starts.**

- Each star is born, goes through its life cycle, and then dies. Stars do not really live. We use the word *living* to talk about how each star begins and ends.
- All stars begin as a nebula. A **nebula** is a large cloud of gas and dust. A nebula spreads out over a huge area of space.
- Gravity pulls gas and dust in a nebula together into a **protostar**. A protostar is a beginning star.
- Nuclear fusion happens when atoms combine and energy is released. In the sun, for example, hydrogen atoms combine to form helium.

Answer the following questions. Use your textbook and the ideas above.

1. Circle the letter of the force that pulls a nebula together into a protostar.
   a. friction
   b. gravity
   c. electricity

2. Circle the letter of what happens when atoms combine in the process of nuclear fusion in a star.
   a. a star dies
   b. gravity pulls a nebula together
   c. energy is released

3. Read each word in the box. In each sentence below, fill in one of the words.

protostar	supernova	nebula

a. A large cloud of gas and dust in space is called a

_______________________.

b. A beginning star is called a

_______________________.

***Key Concept:* How long a star lives depends on its mass.**

- Stars with less mass live longer than stars with more mass. Stars with less mass than the sun can live up to 200 billion years.
- Stars with mass equal to the sun live for about 10 billion years.
- A star with a mass 15 times the mass of the sun may live only about 10 million years.

Answer the following questions. Use your textbook and the ideas above.

4. How long a star lives depends on its

_______________________.

5. Is the following sentence true or false? Stars with more mass live longer than stars with less mass. __________

6. Circle the letter of how long the sun is likely to live.

a. 10 million years

b. 10 billion years

c. 200 billion years

Deaths of Stars (pages 610–613)

***Key Concept:* After a star runs out of fuel, it becomes a white dwarf, a neutron star, or a black hole.**

- Stars with low mass and medium mass eventually run out of fuel. These stars turn into white dwarfs. A **white dwarf** is the blue-white center of a star that is left after the star cools.
- A star with a high mass has a different life cycle than a star with a low mass. When a high-mass star runs out of fuel, it explodes. The explosion of a high-mass star is called a **supernova**.
- After a high-mass star explodes, some of the star is left. This material may form a neutron star. A **neutron star** is the leftover remains of a high-mass star.
- A **pulsar** is a rapidly spinning neutron star.
- The stars with the greatest mass become black holes when they die. A **black hole** is an object with very strong gravity that does not give off any light. A black hole has gravity so strong that nothing escapes its pull—not even light.

Answer the following questions. Use your textbook and the ideas above.

7. Draw a line from each term to its meaning.

Term	**Meaning**
white dwarf	**a.** the blue-white center of a low-mass or medium-mass star that is left after the star cools
supernova	**b.** an object with very strong gravity that does not give off any light
neutron star	**c.** the explosion of a high-mass star
black hole	**d.** the leftover remains of a high-mass star

8. A black hole has so much ______________ that nothing escapes its pull.

9. Read each word in the box. In each blank in the flowchart below, fill in the correct word or words.

Black hole	White dwarf	Protostar

Red giant or supergiant

Stars with small and medium mass → **a.** ______________

Stars with high mass → Supernova

Most massive → **b.** ______________

High mass → Neutron star

Star Systems and Galaxies

(pages 614–618)

Star Systems and Clusters (pages 615–616)

Key Concept: **Most stars are members of groups of two or more stars, called star systems.**

- A star system is a group of two or more stars. A star system that has two stars is called a double star or a **binary star**.
- An **eclipsing binary** is a star system with two stars. In an eclipsing binary, one of the stars sometimes blocks the light from the other star.
- Astronomers have discovered more than 100 planets around other stars.
- Many stars belong to larger groups of stars called star clusters. An **open cluster** is a group of stars that is loose and disorganized. A **globular cluster** is a group of stars that is round and densely packed.

Answer the following questions. Use your textbook and the ideas above.

1. A group of two or more stars is called a star ______________________.

2. Is the following sentence true or false? Astronomers have discovered more than 100 planets around other stars. __________

3. Complete the table about star systems.

Star Systems	
Type of Star System	**Description**
Binary star	two stars
a. ____________________ ____________________	two stars with one star blocking the light of the other
b. ____________________ ____________________	loose and disorganized group of stars
c. ____________________ ____________________	round and densely packed group of stars

Galaxies (page 617)

A galaxy is a huge group of single stars, star systems, star clusters, dust, and gas bound together by gravity.

- There are billions of **galaxies** in the universe.
- Galaxies seem to occur in clusters. Our galaxy, the Milky Way, is part of a cluster of about 50 galaxies called the **Local Group**.

Answer the following questions. Use your textbook and the ideas above.

4. A huge group of stars held together by gravity is a(an) ____________________.

5. The Milky Way is part of a cluster of about 50 galaxies called the ____________________.

Types of Galaxies (page 618)

Key Concept: **Astronomers classify most galaxies into the following types: spiral, elliptical, and irregular.**

- A **spiral galaxy** has a bulge in the middle and arms that curve outward. Most new stars in a spiral galaxy are found in its spiral arms.
- An **elliptical galaxy** looks like a round or flattened ball. Most elliptical galaxies contain only old stars.
- An **irregular galaxy** does not have any certain shape. Irregular galaxies are usually smaller than other types of galaxies. Most irregular galaxies contain many young stars and lots of gas and dust to form new stars.

Answer the following questions. Use your textbook and the ideas above.

6. Astronomers classify galaxies into ______________ groups.

7. Look at the picture below. Then circle the letter of the kind of galaxy the picture shows.

a. spiral galaxy

b. elliptical galaxy

c. irregular galaxy

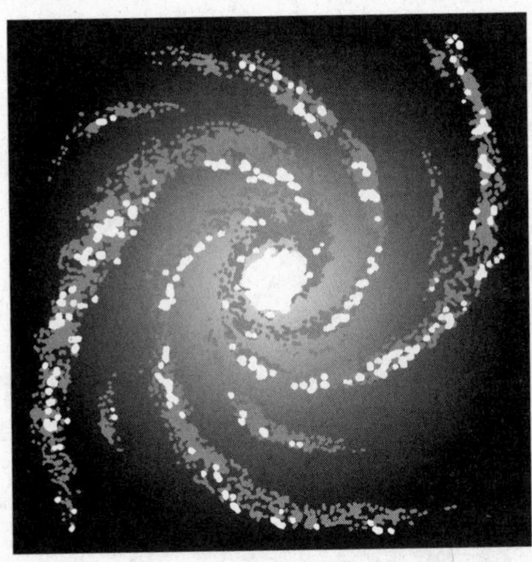

8. Draw a line from each term to its meaning.

Term	**Meaning**
spiral galaxy	**a.** galaxy that does not have any certain shape
elliptical galaxy	**b.** galaxy with a bulge in the middle and arms that curve
irregular galaxy	**c.** galaxy that looks like a round or flattened ball

The Milky Way (page 619)

***Key Concept:* Our solar system is located in a spiral galaxy called the Milky Way.**

- Earth, the sun, and the rest of the solar system are all part of the Milky Way galaxy.
- The Milky Way is a spiral galaxy. Earth is inside one of the galaxy's spiral arms.
- The center of the Milky Way galaxy is about 25,000 light-years from Earth.

Answer the following questions. Use your textbook and the ideas above.

9. Earth is in the galaxy called the

______________________.

10. Circle the letter of the type of galaxy that the Milky Way is.

a. spiral galaxy
b. elliptical galaxy
c. irregular galaxy

The Scale of the Universe (pages 620–621)

Key Concept: **Since the numbers astronomers use are often very large or very small, they frequently use scientific notation to describe sizes and distances in the universe.**

- The **universe** is all of space and everything in space.
- Astronomers study very large things, such as galaxies. Astronomers also study very small things, such as atoms within stars.
- **Scientific notation** is a way of writing large numbers in a short way. Scientific notation uses powers of 10. Each number is written as a number times 10 and a power of 10. For example, consider the number 1,200. Using scientific notation, that number is written like this: 1.2×10^3.

Answer the following questions. Use your textbook and the ideas above.

11. All of space and everything in space is the ______________________.

12. Circle the letter of a number written in scientific notation.

a. 3.43578

b. 1.2×10^3

c. $1.2 \div 10^5$

The Expanding Universe (pages 622–627)

How the Universe Formed (pages 622–624)

***Key Concept:* According to the big bang theory, the universe formed in an instant, billions of years ago, in an enormous explosion.**

- Astronomers' explanation for the start of the universe is called the big bang theory.
- According to the big bang theory, the universe was at first very hot and very small. It was no larger than a period at the end of a sentence. The universe then exploded. That explosion is called the **big bang**. The big bang happened billions of years ago.
- Since the big bang, the universe has been expanding—growing in size.
- Astronomers estimate that the universe is about 13.7 billion years old.

Answer the following questions. Use your textbook and the ideas above.

1. The explosion that formed the universe is called the

   ______________________.

2. Circle the letter of each sentence that is true about the big bang theory.

   a. The universe was at first very cool and very large.

   b. The big bang happened billions of years ago.

   c. The universe was at first very hot and very small.

3. Is the following sentence true or false? Since the big bang, the universe has been expanding. __________

Formation of the Solar System (page 625)

***Key Concept:* About five billion years ago, a giant cloud of gas and dust collapsed to form our solar system.**

- A **solar nebula** is a large cloud of gas and dust in space. A solar nebula was the beginning of our solar system.
- Gravity pulled the solar nebula together. The sun was born.
- Gas and dust gathered together in the outer parts of the disk to form planetesimals. A **planetesimal** was like an asteroid. Over time, planetesimals joined together and became the planets.

Answer the following questions. Use your textbook and the ideas above.

4. Read each word in the box. In each sentence below, fill in the correct word or words.

planetesimals	solar flare	solar nebula

a. A ______________________ is a large cloud of gas and dust in space.

b. Asteroid-like bodies that joined together and became planets were ______________________.

5. Circle the letter of what the solar nebula formed.

a. the solar system

b. the Milky Way galaxy

c. the universe

The Future of the Universe (pages 626–627)

Key Concept: **New observations lead many astronomers to conclude that the universe will likely expand forever.**

- No one knows what will happen to the universe in the future. Many astronomers think that the universe will continue to expand.
- Astronomers think that most of the universe is dark matter. **Dark matter** is matter that does not give off electromagnetic radiation. Because visible light is part of electromagnetic radiation, dark matter cannot be seen.
- Galaxies seem to be moving apart faster than they used to move. Astronomers think that the force moving the galaxies is called **dark energy**.
- Most of the universe is made up of dark matter and dark energy.

Answer the following questions. Use your textbook and the ideas above.

6. Is the following sentence true or false? Dark matter cannot be seen. __________

7. Read each word in the box. In each sentence below, fill in the correct words.

dark energy	dark matter	dark hole

a. Matter that does not give off electromagnetic radiation is called ____________________.

b. Astronomers think that the force moving the galaxies is called ____________________.